Ethnologia Europaea

Journal of European Ethnology

Volume 41:2
2011

MUSEUM TUSCULANUM PRESS · UNIVERSITY OF COPENHAGEN

Printed in Sweden by Grahns Tryckeri AB, Lund 2011
Cover and layout Pernille Sys Hansen
Cover photo Peter Jan Margry, September 2010
At the end of the Santiago trail to Finisterra, "Land's End", pilgrims leave their clothes as a ritual of finishing their journey.
ISBN 978 87 635 3877 0
ISSN 0425 4597

This journal is published with the support of the Nordic board for periodicals in the humanities and social sciences.

Museum Tusculanum Press
University of Copenhagen
Njalsgade 126
DK-2300 Copenhagen S
www.mtp.dk

CONTENTS

CIVIL RELIGION IN EUROPE
Silent Marches, Pilgrim Treks and Processes of Mediatization

Peter Jan Margry

This contribution demonstrates that in relation to societal crises and personal existential anxieties new varieties of religious practice and experience have gained importance in Europe. Based on the analysis of two recent rituals of movement and contemplation – the Dutch silent march and pilgrim treks in Europe – I have sought to uncover manifestations of civil religion. Arising in societies under threat, both ritual forms represent in their mediatized expression alternative public theologies centered around an ideal of a society at peace and possessing moral unity. It is this mediatization of these crisis rituals that gives them a meaning beyond itself, offering a moral and spiritual frame of reference for both European society as a whole and for its citizens individually.

Keywords: civil religion, crisis rituals, anxiety, memorialization, heritage, mediatization

Since 1967, when Robert Bellah proposed his renowned model of a transcendent civil religion as a universal belief system within American society, the concept of civil religion has largely been perceived as an American phenomenon (cf. Bellah & Hammond 1980; Kim 1993). Originally triggered by constitutional rituals and commemorative practices within the United States, the enlightenment idea of a civil religion was given new meanings by the theorizing and critiques of a series of American sociologists (Bellah, Coleman, Richey, Gehrig, Hammond, Jones, Wimberley etc.), resulting in the construction of an "American Civil Religion" (Mathisen 1989). In the words of Christenson and Wimberley, it is an ideological social construct differentiated from "common religion", being neither a reduction of Christian principles to essentials, nor a synthesis of religious pluralism or the politicization of religion. They see the basic tenets of American civil religion as "the perception of Divine sanctions and inherent morality in civil laws" and the ascription of sacred connotations to secular symbols and practices (1978: 77).

Notwithstanding the many publications on the theme, many of Bellah's initial postulates basically still stand, and have indeed taken root elsewhere. His remark that "all politically organized societies have some sort of civil religion" (Bellah 1974: 257) has also drawn the attention of researchers outside the United States to the subject (Kleger & Müller 1986). In the past decade a renewed interest in the manifestations of civil religion in Europe has become apparent, unfolding perspectives on civil religion outside the US realm (cf. Davie 2001; Parsons 2002; Kleger & Müller 2004; Hvithamar, Warburg & Jacobsen 2009). In that context the rise of (cultural) nationalism in twentieth-century Europe fed the idea that even nationalism should be interpreted as the (civil) religion of modern times – a view which, however, has also been subject to criticism (Santiago 2009).[1] As the academic field of civil religion had mainly been explored on a theoretical level and showed a substantial lack of empirical data, European ethnologists and anthropologists commenced trying to identify civil religion on a more ethnographic basis, employing a more open conceptual paradigm (Rawbottom 2001; Margry 2008b; Barna 2009; Povedák 2009).

In this contribution I will elaborate on this basis and seek to adapt it to a more general concept of civil religion with which contemporary rituality can be interpreted in new ways. The concept is not operationalized as a fixed target but as a paradigm in order to understand and explain what is happening and why the researched phenomena are so popular and subsequently so widely mediatized. In this light I hope the results also add to the ongoing discussion on the concept of civil religion itself.[2] For this article I studied pilgrim treks in Europe and silent marches in the Netherlands for which I analyzed a vast amount of media messages and articles, (published) pilgrim diaries, interviews and questionnaires.[3]

John Coleman already made a rather convincing effort toward a synthetic open definition of civil religion (Coleman 1970: 69–70). Based on his interpretation, and leaving the specific American-national focus out, my operational definition is as follows: civil religion is the religious symbol system which relates the citizen's role and society's place in space, time and history to the conditions of ultimate existence and meaning.[4] For Europe the last part of this definition is nowadays particularly relevant as, partly due to the undermined position of institutionalized religion, traumatic death and its memorialization have become oversensitive and major issues, as we can infer from new mourning practices, which even have been termed "memorial mania" (Doss 2010: 2; cf. Margry & Sánchez-Carretero 2011). Although my stance derives from Durkheim's implicit definition of civil religion (cf. Durkheim [1912]2001: 25–46) and its ascribed quality to integrate and create community, this perspective should not be taken as an all-inclusive model (cf. Cottle 2006: 428). Included among the cases presented here are some in which divisive and conflict-oriented tendencies are present, which exclude individuals or religious or ethnic subgroups in the way Gamoran for example found exclusion in American schools (Gamoran 1990: 254). The "noise wake" after the murder of movie director Theo van Gogh in Amsterdam in 2004 is an example of that, a contrarious ritual, as Van Gogh disliked "bourgeois", consensus-driven silent marches – but see also the postings by others (often young people) who say they have "silent march fatigue", or regard the silent march as outdated and/or not functional.[5] Nevertheless, as I will demonstrate, the case studies treated are characterized by a dominant but not comprehensive community-creating quality. Moreover, do such rituals, as Lane argued, mirror problematic social relations or political concerns, and do they help sacralizing the social order (Lane 1981)?

For the argument in this article I have shifted my focus from state-organized rituals to non-institutionalized ritual practices of individuals and grassroots civil organizations in society. In that line, elaborating on Grace Davie's open theory of "Global Civil Religion" from a European perspective,[6] and to facilitate research into emerging practices and patterns, I would like to revise the concept in two ways: by making it more universal, detached from the "nationalistic" American situation, and also by stretching the concept into a supranational dimension, in this case the European realm. This will be demonstrated and elaborated on the basis of two very different examples of civic rituality that have the potential to generate civil religion. Their dissimilarity makes it clear that civil religion is not just to be found in those practices with which it is usually connected, but that research should examine other less obvious rituals and practices that in themselves do not obviously express civil religion.

On the other hand, what these two examples do have in common is that they are "locally" constituted rituals of movement, and performed in public. It is only through a transfer process realized by the media that they gain their generic civil quality. It is through the intervention of the media that the examples are generalized to a (trans)national or European level. To explain this I need to introduce and focus on the role of modern processes of mediatization. Major researchers on this theme endorse the assumption that the mediatization of rituals serves to sustain and/or mobilize collective sentiments and solidarities on the basis of symbolization and a subjective orientation to what should or ought to be, as Cottle defined it (Cottle 2006: 415). Lundby relates mediatization more to societal changes and the role of media and mediated communication in these transformations of society (2009: 1). Moreover, in the case of a small European democracy similar to the Netherlands (i.e., Denmark) Hjarvard found that media are effective agents of religious change, distributors of Christian-inspired values and norms "providing both moral and spiritual guidance and a sense of community" (Hjarvard 2008: 24). Such agency does not seem limited to those examples, but as an active factor it is applicable in a more generic way in European society.

The particular quality of modern media as the primary conduit for communication of messages and symbols clarifies that the practiced ritual and symbol language presented only create a full range of effect, and can only be transformed into civil religion when, with the use of mass media like TV and the Internet, they are transferred from the local to the (supra)national level. Media then have a "social integrative function" and play "a vital role in the ritualization of important societal transitions," with which whole communities can, for example, participate in collective mourning and coping with trauma, as Hjarvard argues (2008: 18–20). Using the definition given above, I will first demonstrate that the popular Dutch grassroots crisis ritual, the silent march, has the capacity to become civil religion when its performative power is nationally disseminated by the media. This performativity does not imply just the local enactment of the ritual, but also includes the active commitment of an audience at distance, which is prepared to "participate" in a symbolically meaningful way (cf. Cottle 2006: 428–29). Second, I will indicate how a less nation-state orientated approach is also needed within civil religion studies in order to identify supranational forms of civil religion, as in the case of the revived pan-European practice of treks on pilgrim ways.

The Silent March as Crisis Ritual

On October 22, 2002, in the Dutch city of Venlo, a 22-year-old man, René Steegmans, saw two teenagers on a motor scooter narrowly miss clipping an elderly woman. He shouted to them to show more respect for their elders. With this, both teenagers turned on him and began to beat and kick him so severely that he died of his injuries shortly after. In the eyes of the Dutch populace such expressions of violence had increased significantly over the previous decade, and were seen in part as an expression of an individualized and multi-cultural society that prevented assimilation of new ethnic and religious groups, and in turn resulted in rising pressures on "living together", and caused social norms and values to become blurred and faded away. The term "senseless violence" came into use to apply to these very serious forms of aggression for which there does not seem to be any apparent reason (cf. Pouwels & Vegter 2002). This is a form of violence that is regarded as all the more evil because one cannot assign any justified meaning or function to it. Because such violence for the sake of violence, from boredom, perversity or arising from alcohol abuse, is more or less incomprehensible for civil society, and can occur at any time without any clear cause, not only are its consequences extremely traumatic for the families of victims, but the phenomenon also challenges the traditional, ostensibly peaceful image and high value standards that the Dutch keep of their society. The case in Venlo fed this thinking still further because it sparked off a national debate after the parents of the primary perpetrator, a Moroccan-Dutch boy, declared on television that their son was only "an instrument who carried out the will of Allah." The statement divided the Moroccan-Dutch community itself, but chiefly appeared to highlight the shortcomings of the national integration process and to stress the problems Western society is facing with regard to the impact of Islamic culture and religion and the role of the media in the changing perceptions of Islamic culture in relation to violence.

In order to allow people to mourn collectively, to discharge some of the tension in the atmosphere of crisis, and to promote cohesion in the divided communities in the city, three days later a silent march was held in which 17,000 people, among them different Moroccan groups, took part, out of a total population of 90,000 residents (Visser 2002). It was an exceptional ritual broadcast all over the country. In Cottle's taxonomy this phenomenon could be identified as a combination of "moral panic" and "mediatized public crisis": the mobilization of collective fears and anxieties in concurrence with the manifestation of social drama (Cottle 2006: 416). Through the nationwide media attention a national idea of unity and alarm against senseless violence and the dangers of Islam was realized, meanwhile the online condolence registers had to be closed down because of many anti-Moroccan racist postings.

Since the 1990s the collective public manifestation that in Dutch is termed a *stille tocht*, or silent march, has become a general and widely accepted ritual in crisis situations (Post et al. 2003: 79–186). This ritual, which takes place precisely in times of social turbulence, has acquired a place as a prototype in national observance and memorialization practice and has, based on a proven ritual tradition, the power to enhance societal cohesion and reduce societal tension. This march distinguishes itself from public parading by football fans or other communal public manifestations because of its ratio as coping ritual in cases of trauma and situations of existential crisis. The symbol system is one in direct connection to life and death, represented in processional community finding, an explicit wording during the commemorative and, eventually, the creation of a temporary memorial.

Crisis Ritual in Transformation

The present silent march has its roots in the sixteenth century when the Netherlands became religiously mixed as a result of the Reformation, and remained divided. In the newly created Protestant Republic of the Seven United Provinces Roman Catholics were as a consequence forbidden to express their faith publicly. The importance of procession practice in the Catholic culture of devotion and remembrance, led Catholics to seek ways to keep this traditional veneration practice alive in a non-ostentatious manner that would be tolerated by the Protestant authorities. They invented a rudimentary "procession", not performed as solemn liturgical ceremony, but individually without any religious symbols or sounds, that would follow the former sacred trajectories.[7]

The successful emancipation of Dutch Catholics in the nineteenth century was followed by an initiative on the part of the Catholics to be permitted more open manifestations of their faith in public. Around 1900 the ritual of individual silent processions was "reconstructed" into yearly large-scale collective marches, still silent and without any religious symbols. The silent procession of Amsterdam developed in the twentieth century into the most successful periodic celebration of Dutch Catholicism. It proved to be an effective instrument to increase cohesion within the Catholic diaspora and create Catholic nationalism in a newly imagined community. In its low-key performance the ritual was also generally perceived as an implicit protest march against the restrictions the Catholics still faced (Caspers & Margry 2006: 41–56).

The shared experience of the humiliation of the Dutch nation during the Second World War and the suffering that the whole people underwent weakened the traditional barriers of the rigid social-religious segmentation of Dutch society of those days, and led to a certain (if temporary) postwar sense of religious reconciliation. This made possible that the old Catholic ritual of the silent procession became the template for the national and multifaith yearly observance and memorialization of the victims of the Second World War. On 4 May, 1946, the national Remembrance Day, 600 cities and towns organized a silent march for the first time, with hundreds of thousands of participants in total. The silent memorial marches were an immediate success. This new minimalistic commemorative ritual in collective form was described as "serene, spiritual and dignified", but at the same time intended also to express a moral intention. The central idea behind the silent marches was the desire that arose after the war to generate hope and inspiration for a better future, and to arrive at a "strengthening of solidarity" and cohesion on a national level. In most communities where a march took place, it developed into a ritual of personal and collective reconciliation that aided in processing the national trauma associated with the war, and at the same time was an immanent protest against war and violence in general. Participants regarded it as an indirect protest: "this [i.e., the war] must never happen again" (Caspers & Margry 2006: 59). Although organized locally, it was primarily a national commemoration, mediatized likewise. Years later the purpose of the marches would be expanded to include remembrance of victims of all hostilities in which the Netherlands had ever been involved, and they further assumed the function of being a symbolic protest against injustice and discrimination in general.

The success of the annual memorial marches can be explained through its nature as a neutral, basic and therefore accessible ritual in which all denominations of the so strongly divided ("pillarized") Netherlands could easily participate, not only individuals but also representative members of the national community. Immediately after the first memorial march in 1946 newspaper articles mentioned the euphoria of those present, who greatly appreciated the "sense of [national] unity" which the ritual as a form of *communitas* proved to be able to create in the Netherlands (Caspers & Margry 2006: 60).

Later, in the 1960s, a "new" type of march arose out of the silent memorial march, which can more specifically be called the silent march of protest. It hardly differed in terms of form, but had a different function.[8] The two types of silent march existed alongside one another, and were an antithesis to the noisy protest demonstration that made a massive appearance in those days. The silent marches came to be employed increasingly widely as an instrument of protest, against ongoing or new wars, against oppressive regimes, and after the deaths of exceptional international figures. The phenomenon also appeared very occasionally in other countries, such as the march after the murder of Martin Luther King. While until the early 1990s the silent march was still particularly directed as a stand against the violence of warfare, it began to be increasingly used against rising racism in the Netherlands, such as the silent march on August 16, 1992, in response to the shooting of a young Moroccan-Dutch boy due to racist motives, or the vandalism of a Jewish cemetery in Middelburg in 1993.

These were the first signals of another transformation in the silent march ritual. As a "last" developmental phase, a more frequent, structured and an almost generally accepted moral ritual arose alongside and out of the more politically focused silent protest marches, which is today what in the Netherlands would commonly be identified as *the* silent march. The term for the genre has now become the proper noun denoting such events: the silent march. In the second half of the 1990s these marches evolved into the widely accepted mourning and crisis ritual after traumatic death, as it is familiarly known in the Netherlands today. To date, more than hundred of these silent marches have taken place.

The first massive, and thus in a certain sense constitutive, silent march was the memorial march that was held after an El Al Boeing jet freighter crashed into a large apartment complex in the Bijlmermeer, an Amsterdam immigrant neighborhood, on October 4, 1992, while attempting an emergency landing at Schiphol airport. This incident is one of the major catastrophes in recent Dutch history. The magnitude of the disaster, the estimated amount of at least 43 victims, and the trauma it raised on dwellers along all urban airport approach routes, enhanced the need for a nationwide commemoration. One week after the crash a silent march was held in which 40,000 people participated, and proved to be a successful format to help overcome the grief and trauma in which people of 36 different nationalities – and actually the whole nation – were involved.

This disaster and the "first" racist or "senseless" (Dutch: *zinloos*) killing, the stabbing of the Antillean-Dutch teenager Kerwin Duinmeijer by a sixteen-year-old skinhead in 1983, might be seen as constitutive traumas for Dutch society, and might explain why these are the only ones which are still being kept memorialized with a recurrent annual silent march.[9]

Although in the 1990s there were still silent marches of an international and "political" character, held against dictators such as Suharto (August 19, 1996), as a memorial for the massacre in Srebrenica, Bosnia (July 11, 1996), for victims of terrorism, or to commemorate the Kristallnacht in 1938 (November 10, 1997) et cetera, the silent march became more and more synonymous with the ritual for civilian victims in the Netherlands itself.[10] The definitive confirmation of the transformation of the ritual came with the death of Meindert Tjoelker on September 13, 1997, another victim of what in the Netherlands is termed "senseless violence".[11] During a bachelor party outing, the week before his marriage, the 30-year-old Meindert was kicked to death by four men who were vandalizing bicycles, after he had ordered them to stop. In part because his victimization assumed almost mythic proportions in Dutch media, this event established the ritual format of the silent march as reserved purely for cases of senseless violence and after disasters. Since then the ritual has been part of the national mourning repertoire. If the trauma of the fatal loss, and perhaps still more definitive, if the trauma of the way in which this loss occurred is great enough, it seems to be a rule that a silent march will be organized, although the mechanism is not always clear. The story of the "senseless" death of Tjoelker became a newly constructed format on which many marches were based: a "mythical" narrative, stripped of its context, that recounts the event in a reductionist way as a battle between good and evil, while a reconstruction of the events brought up a much more complicated situation (Pouwels & Vegter 2002: 22).

Notwithstanding the early example of Kerwin Duinmeijer mentioned above, victims of immigrant background initially received less media attention as examples of what was perceived as senseless violence, as compared with native Dutch casualties. After 2000 this difference disappeared and organizing a march also became part of the grassroots immigrant culture (cf. Vasterman 2001; Stengs 2007).

It is nowadays unthinkable that a silent march would be called to reinforce the salary demands of the police during pay negotiations, as still happened in 1995. A silent march which was held by friends of animals for a dog that died as a result of neglect and abuse by its owner created general indignation, because it was seen as a trivialization and a profanation of a ritual that should be reserved for human victims in particularly tragic circumstances (Van Dijk 1999).

The silent march as a long, basic procession of people did not remain entirely unchanged. While the given concept on which the marches were based was to proceed in complete silence, in a calm and dignified manner, without having attention-seeking texts or attributes, in recent years flyers or objects have sometimes been tacitly introduced. They are carried along by individuals, and sometimes even the silence will be broken. It may also happen that participants carry texts which agitate against what happened or against the situation which allowed it to occur. With increasing frequency groups also allow themselves to be spurred on at particular moments, often at the end of the march, to chant slogans or to sing together, to press home their cause. The tension that the emotional silence generates appears to require some form of discharge, and on very rare occasions this has happened literally with the use of fireworks at the end of the march. Not only texts on banners, but also balloons and torches are attributes that are appearing with silent marches. Because the beginning or end points of the marches are often places where the person(s) being remembered died, or is buried, participants may bring along something to leave there – flowers, toys, letters or cuddly stuffed animals – and create a temporary memorial in the way as they are made for traffic victims (cf. Everett 2002).

A Performative Ritual

The silent march, as it is commonly termed in the Netherlands, is first and foremost a grassroots collective expression of grief and mourning over what has happened to or overcome a person or group. The grief is shared with the relatives of the victim or victims, but also with all those others who feel themselves affected in one way or another (friends, neighbors, fellow residents of a city, fellow sufferers, etc.). Although initially often instigated by the local authorities, they are now usually organized by the victim's family, acquaintances, colleagues or neighbors, sometimes with the assistance of local victim services or antiracism groups, etc. Its form is a long procession of people, often led by family members and representatives of local (and in the case of greater disasters, also national) administrations, politics, churches, et cetera. As a rule these massive mourning marches are also an expression of widely shared feelings of moral indignation, addressed to the Dutch government or society as a whole. Lynn posted the online message "I hope the march empowers you all; show that this nonsensical violence must stop."[12] The silent march then delivers a more or less implicit protest against phenomena such as senseless violence and dangerous conditions (particularly involving traffic and transportation) and the traumas which these cause.

The rise and development of the silent march in its present form can be explained by the feelings of disharmony between our ideals and the world as it is. The absolutization of individual freedom has lead to a less social way of living and subsequently a disintegration of community, of which senseless violence is perceived as one of the consequences (cf. Verbrugge 2004: 28). Another explanatory element is the strongly decreased acceptance of premature, illogical or irrational ("senseless") death in modern society. The idea has taken root that in the contemporary, technological, closely regulated world, with the marvels of modern science and medicine, death can be banished to a considerable extent. When people are still confronted by a premature death without rhyme or reason, the grief is all the greater and the grief processing all the more difficult. Relatives then also feel the need to inform the world at large with the "injustice" – "Why you Nathalie?"[13] – that has taken place. The reason for this behavior is twofold. On the one hand it helps the personal coping with the trauma, on the other it involves the outside world in a general healing process for the trauma that was aroused by the disaster.

Participants in the silent march express that they feel united in a national alliance against irrationality and the lack of norms in society. They regard the feelings that exist on this matter in society as being symbolically represented in the march, as the mayor formulated in the Steegmans case: "I think that silence represents yelling; crying out that the government should deal with senseless violence." A journalist described the march: "It is the ritualization of impotence and therefore the only just reaction." A.H. wrote, "I want to participate, because this is senseless violence and it has to stop."[14] Or in the case of the death of Quincy Schumans, an Antillean teenager shot by his best friend, a woman called Mathilde posted, "What does this bring for our Netherlands?"[15] By a performative march they wish to draw attention to these problems at a national level, and appeal both to the authorities and to society itself (and potential perpetrators within it) to help prevent new cases and reinstate central values in and for society; or, as Lodewijkx, Kersten and van Zomeren state, affirming sacred values, solidarity with the moral community and an affiliated belief in a just world (2008: 154, 164). This is typified by the search for collectivity, cohesion and mutual support in society, in word, gesture and ritual, when that society has become too strongly individualistic, and traditional and national communal ties have been undermined, lost, or never developed and the role of the churches is in retreat. The collective march has therefore been qualified as "searching for community" (Jansen 2000: 79) – a vigorous ritual with which the community at the local level, but also through the media at a national level, straightens out with real life again. Sometimes the ritual was therefore also called a "fraternization march". Moreover, with this new public ritual, Dutch society surprised itself by the fact that individuals in a grassroots movement could be mobilized for general societal anxieties.

Time and again the traumatic incidents provoke generic existential feelings of anxiety – this could happen to me (or my child) too – among the general population (cf. Kierkegaard [1844]1980: 41–46). The ritual then indeed expresses the (latent) feelings of the whole community, serving as a prophylactic instrument to exorcise "evil", suppress anxieties and make a public appeal to main-

Ill. 1: Silent march for Quincy Schumans, a Dutch-Antillean sixteen-year-old boy shot by a friend in Amsterdam, September 5, 2010. (Photo: Peter Jan Margry)

tain the norms and values of society. When in 1999 the 16-year-old Marianne Vaatstra was abused and murdered, a mother explained her participation in the silent march – with 15,000 other participants – as follows: "Everyone I know has the strong feeling 'it could have been my child'."[16] In relation to a march for another murdered young woman in 2010, again Lynn wrote: "Respect for the silent march. Show that this nonsensical violence must stop."[17] What struck society, and has since also remained the focus of the media, was this way of "finding community" through marches, an antithetical development to what is generally seen as the process of individualization. This does not however exclude the fact that when a silent march is announced debates will often occur on Internet forums about the functionality of silent marches and the question of them having become obsolete as a means for mourning and protest. Plugge85 wrote: "For the mourning maybe good, but I get fed up with these marches."[18]

This media focus is fundamental for the meaning and reach of the phenomenon of silent marches. Apart from the effects of a silent march at the local level, the cohesive and assuaging power of the civil religion it generates is only realized as a result of intervention by the media, especially the national media. The experience of transcendency of a silent march at a national level is in fact totally dependent of intermediality. Without the presence of the media and their widespread broadcasting and publishing, the marches could not be observed so closely by so many and would consequently not gain their attributed meanings. Even after so many marches, when a traumatic death occurs people organize a silent march, and it will still be covered, almost as a mantra, by the media. Although after more than a decade, the marches' functionality has been disputed (cf. Bijma 2007: 74), with the medial dissemination of their meanings they continue to fulfill their role in recovering the delicate balances regarding emotions and life and death.

Although people in the media also have observed that silent marches do not prevent senseless violence, they are not entirely without any practical influence. This has become clear from the way they have raised political awareness, and the various practical civil and administrative initiatives taken – traffic and public safety measures – as a result of the marches to deal with the social problems the marches address. Also, stimulated by the wide attention that marches against senseless violence and loutishness have gained, the public discussion on norms and values has been placed on the national political agenda. The popularity of silent marches has even turned them into an export product. Since 2000, beginning most prolifically in Belgium, the silent march has become better known in the world as a mourning and protest ritual.[19]

A Unifying March for Civil Society

As mentioned before, the widespread attention given by the media to the phenomenon of silent marches plays a crucial role in bringing the significance and effects of the marches to a national level. Despite the fact that as a rule they are responses to local events by locally organized groups, both spokespersons and commentators insist that, in their perception, these marches represent feelings that are found elsewhere too, nationally and throughout society. The incidents to which these marches are responses are thus presented as typical examples of the decline of the morale of the nation, a lack of oversight by the government or the injustice of life. In these cases the ritual permits the community involved to express itself, and further serves to exorcize the "evil" and to control and redress existential anxieties. In the words of the mayor of Gorinchem, "because it could have happened to any one of us... that understanding affects democracy and the sense of safety" (Bal, van Dijk-Groeneboer & Menken-Bekius 2001: 282). The ritual also makes a public, national appeal for the maintenance of social norms and values in contemporary society – one in which norms and values are believed to have become eroded, and increasingly less able to be identified. The absence of national symbolic moral anchors means that these grassroots initiatives assume an even greater value, and turns them (with a certain governmental encouragement) into an ideological instrument (cf. Christenson & Wimberley 1978: 82).

In the search for these characteristic Dutch norms and values, and *a fortiori* for a new Dutch identity and better society, reference is often made to the Christian roots of the "secularized" nation. This is particularly the case for marches following incidents of senseless violence, when quite often their organizers or spokesmen make explicit reference to the Ten Commandments and the fading away of their observance in individualized modernity, and which, it is suggested, must again be imposed as a moral guide for society. Participants of the marches usually admit that the march helps to control emotionality at the personal and local level, while journalists or sociologists writing in the media state that the collective indignation aroused to certain extent also soothes and conciliates the affected (national) community. The mediatized active participation of people in the street resacralizes ritual and imagination, and thus makes a strong appeal to the national community (cf. Hjarvard 2008: 24). This reassurance then creates a temporary overarching unity in society that can be called civil religion. This does not of course mean that all citizens feel united, but that through the media society at large is involved and coping with the issues raised by the trauma.

Pilgrim Treks in Europe

The second example of civil religion I want to focus on is related to the successful heritage creation and religious renewal that has emerged in recent decades along revitalized pilgrim ways all over Europe. The network of trails seem to have both dynamized Christian roots, capitalizing on the new religious and spiritual demands created by secularization, as well as responding to the demand for shared and Christian-inspired European values and meanings in times of crisis and anxiety.

A renewed interest in "ancient" pilgrimage trails – in particular initially the various European routes to Santiago de Compostela – picked up speed in the 1960s, arising at first from the perspective of the history of art and architecture along the *camino* (Oursel 1963).[20] In the years that followed this focus slowly changed into what today is called the "art of pilgrimage" as a reference to the central significance of pilgrimage, foot routes and contemplative movement in new forms of religiosity. Apart from the centuries-old metaphor that every human life here in this world is a severe and enduring pilgrimage, in individualized modernity pilgrimages are seen more and more as an inquiry and a quest of the self for values and meanings in life, as well as for the understanding of life and its hereafter (e.g., Cousineau 1998; Rupp 2005; Webb-Mitchell 2007).

Because of this process the rationale of pilgrimage has been changing. Its main goal is nowadays often not to be found in the contact with the sacred at the shrine at the end of the road, but in the activity and finality of *doing* the pilgrimage, the actual walking itself – not the sacred destination, for which formerly the walking was only the practical necessity for accomplishment (Margry 2008a: 24–25). Walking, and certainly long distance treks, can be boring and toilsome, but the new endeavor is to apply the art to perform this basic activity in a sublime way. As a combined physical-sensory activity, and connected with the human capacity for reflection, the trekking should create sufficient satisfaction and meaning that deeper thoughts or spiritual experiences will flow from it (Cousineau 1998; George 2006). These experiences will be enhanced when wandering is practiced on tracks that have proven their spiritual relevance. Adherents of new spiritualities thus often travel along the same tracks, to the same spots, as these represent a universal spiritual value to them. A 32-year-old man from Belgium perceived on the camino "a fusion of the 'old' and the 'new' religion, an 'ecumene'; which represents values based on the Ten Commandments, values that are important during your whole life."[21]

It is due to this development in particular that pilgrimage researchers Coleman and Eade drew inspiration from the idea of physical motion in relation to pilgrimage. Embroidering on Hervieu-Léger's *La religion en mouvement* (1999), they identify pilgrimages as "cultures in motion", based on the many testimonies of the spiritual and physical transformation effected by the journey to Santiago and the combination of "travel, pilgrimage and tourism" on the *camino* (Coleman & Eade 2004: 11).

Fieldwork by Albers adds the element that during the pilgrim's journey movement in itself can release forces that are grasped by pilgrims as sacral (Albers 2007: 445–450). Apart from the fact that hiking can also actually be physically healing – as it happens, walking releases hormonal dopamine that help your body and yourself to feel better – it seems that walking also can deepen one spiritually. A female Santiago pilgrim wrote of her journey, "The essence is that you are in search of the sense and absurdity in life. I have learned to put aside my tendency toward rational logic. There is more between heaven and earth."[22] And there are many such statements, as since the 1980s a whole new genre of travel books and reflective diaries and blogs written by Santiago pilgrims has arisen, which can serve as source material yielding ample evidence for this quest (e.g., Frey 1998; Post, Pieper & van Uden 1998: 221–242). According to one of these travelers, walking the pilgrim way is "how to travel outward to the edges of the world while simultaneously journeying to the depths of your soul" (Cousineau 1998: back cover). Still another pilgrim recounted the historical depth of the trails: "On my journey westward along the *camino,* I felt I was traveling backward in time to a place where began the experiences that made me, and the human race what we have become today" (Maclaine 2000: 10). For many walkers the journey along a pilgrim route has become an individual rite of passage, or "a pilgrimage to one's self" as Eberhart once called it (Eberhart 2006: 260). Trekking the pilgrim trails has become an inward-orientated activity for questioning oneself or giving meaning to oneself in relation to the world. But the networks' influence is not just a personal issue, it affects European society as well. Various pilgrims stress the importance of walking pilgrim ways as a "binding" and "fraternizing" practice, which "creates mutual understanding" among themselves and *a fortiori* among the people and nations of Europe.[23]

Walking the pilgrim ways today, one at the same time reaches back to the wanderings of the early missionaries, who by their *peregrinatio* gave shape to the spiritual "grand tour" of the early Middle Ages (Kötting 1950; Bitton-Ashkelony 2005). It was with their pilgrim wanderings that Christian thought was broadly dynamized for the first time and spread across Europe as culture and religion. Today this is happening anew. Hervieu-Léger formulated the useful concept of the "chain of memory and tradition", with which we also in this case can explain how through the pilgrim-trail network European heritage and Christian values are again being revitalized and mobilized in the collective memory. The *camino* is the metaphor for Christianity which serves as an ideological and symbolic device with which European identity is created anew, and which makes individuals and European society at large aware of belonging to a religious lineage or tradition. In this way the network has become a supranational vehicle with which various connections are realized in newly constructed spiritual and heritage-based imagined communities (Hervieu-Léger 2000: 171–177; cf. Davie 2001: 465–468). These communities find inspiration from the past in creating new forms of religiosity which may also help individuals cope with their problems, insecurities and doubts (cf. Peelen & Jansen 2007), but also strongly reconfirm Christian roots and values in their public and mediatized form in contemporary multicultural European society. Just as the Dutch silent march is related to a specific incident but has more general effects, the pilgrimage also helps to resolve the concerns of the pilgrim – or better, the community – in a more general way, with regard to a process that is perceived as a sense of being uprooted as a result of trends in modern society. It is an instrumentalization of the religious past in a new ideology, which was defined by Hobsbawm as the recurrent process that he called inventing traditions or "practices, normally governed by overtly of tacitly accepted rules and of a ritual or symbolic nature, which seek to inculcate certain values and norms of behaviour by repetition, which automatically implies continuity with the past" (Hobsbawm 1983: 1). This process includes not only the performative practice of pilgrimaging, but also the new routes themselves, which for the most part have been invented and newly constructed. This development was so successful that through the heritage creation of and on the routes the pilgrim treks have become more and more disconnected from contemporary institutional religion and its troubled political and social connotations. Although some pilgrims mentioned the violent past of the Catholic Church, most recognized the importance of Christian culture and its values. As two Dutch pilgrims wrote: "Our European culture and identity are based on it"; "we have no other/better values."[24]

Without the extensive and widespread media coverage of the old pilgrimage practices, the cultural politics of Spain, Unesco and of the European Union, the transition from a destination-oriented ritual to seeing the journey as a pilgrimage in itself would not have been so universal, as it is now. Nowadays pilgrimages have no starting point and destination – or at any rate they are not relevant. Being detached from daily life, moving, walking, the accessibility and freedom of the ritual, time for reflection and contemplation, being in nature, and tranquility are all elements that have contributed to its success.

The success of the spiritual format related to the transnational network of pilgrims' tracks leading to Santiago, in combination with their art, culture, antiquity and their contemporary revitalization, also brought the camino to the attention of supranational organizations. Because the strong dynamics of the network propagated and enhanced Christian culture in Europe, even as it had in the Middle Ages, the European Union recognized the significance of the pilgrimage ways early on. The potential of such a value-creating network, which moreover was supranational in character, dovetailed perfectly with European political ambitions (Schrire 2006: 69–72). In 1987, less than a year after Spain had become a member of the EU and – important for pilgrims – open borders had come into effect, this led to the Council of Europe proclaiming the Camino to Santiago de Compostela the first European Cultural Itinerary. This high status was further upgraded in 1993 through its inclusion on the Unesco World Heritage list. With that listing it was established that the camino had "outstanding universal value" as a logistic system – thus not because of the static historic material culture along the route, but chiefly because of the fundamental role of the route in "encouraging cultural exchanges between the Iberian peninsula and *the rest of Europe* during the Middle Ages" – and, I would add, also after the Middle Ages. Or, as the Unesco site has it, "it remains a testimony to the power of the Christian faith among people of all social classes and from all over Europe." This is the appreciation of intangible heritage in its performative dimensions. But every bit as much, the recognition is a canonization of the rediscovered Christian pilgrimage as an instrument of trans-European cohesive force. Quantitatively this resonates in the numbers of Santiago pilgrims, which have grown steadily from 2,905 in 1987 to 269,742 in 2010, figures which represent only the officially counted pilgrims, who indeed arrived in Santiago.[25] This promotion of the pilgrim ways is nowadays an ideological instrument to facilitate the stability of the European political system, a "manipulation" like that found by Christenson and Wimberley for civil religion in America (1978: 82), inspired by Christianity.

The fascination of spiritual seekers remains deep, and the engagement of the organizations behind it at such a high level that in addition to the Spanish-French camino similar routes were sought, found and, if necessary, created ex nihilo all over Europe (Döring [2003]2004: 54). In relation to Connerton's view, it is clear that the images of past pilgrimage and the recollected knowledge about it are conveyed and sustained by a modern ritual performance of the new pilgrims (Connerton 1989: 39–40). The construction of a mythical network of trans-European pilgrim ways as part of the historical camino to Santiago reflects thus how Europe is imagined as a thoroughly Christian subcontinent, and how Christian heritage is being reinvented. A 58-year-old man from the Netherlands stated that the Christian camino reflects the "norms and values we cherish" in Europe.[26] The pilgrimage itineraries form one of the implicit answers to Europe's confusion about religion and spirituality in general, and symbolically and practically reposition Christianity in an ecumenical or neutral way as a unifying historical factor.[27] This idea is splendidly explored and endorsed by Sven Grabow's study of Europe's cultural policy on the routes to Santiago. An assessment of the Polish and the Danish routes, for example, clearly demonstrates its missionary character and the strategy of bringing in Christian heritage to this Santiago route, as only 16 percent of the heritage along the track has a relation to Saint James (Grabow 2010: 97–99). The track thus actually revolves more around Christianity in general, and expresses an ideologically fed Christian discourse. Grabow states that the pilgrim paths, underpinned by instrumentalizing "evidence", develop "a pan-European cultural heritage paradigm characterized by closedness, exclusivity, and homogeneity" (Grabow 2010: 108). Subsequently pilgrim treks propagate this grammar of Christianity among the public, and it is disseminated further by the media. This performative activity helps in re-establishing the community's fading historic norms and values.

Thus, in this case too mediatization plays a central role in spreading and dynamizing the idea of trans-European spiritual paths. It is a form of Christian transnationalism, the strengthening of a pan-European identity, against the backdrop of the eclipse of transnational Christian Democracy in Europe (cf. Davie 2001: 466–67). It is also a reaction to the increasing tensions regarding the separation of church and state, and the increasing presence of Islam and other faiths in Europe.

Today, the wide interest in pilgrimage routes and the decisive role attributed to the many revitalized and new pilgrimage trails to Santiago, the *Via Francigena* to Rome, "les chemins de Saint Martin de Tours", the Austrian "Spiritual Path", the Dutch "Pelgrimswegen", the "European Path of Contemplation" and many others,[28] have extended beyond the domain of cultural heritage and the open religious domain. The Catholic Church itself has also begun to focus more strongly on the meaning of the journey than on the cult object (Saint James) at the final destination. Whereas formerly the walking journey was a necessary evil, nowadays it is seen as "tradition" or as pilgrimage heritage, and more and more frequently a pilgrimage is only seen as a "real" pilgrimage if it is completed on foot and on an "historical" way. Special Catholic and secular travel agencies have come into being to help individuals on their way. Dedicated national Saint James associations, often counting more than 10,000 members, deal with the pre- and post-camino social, practical and spiritual care of pilgrims and potential pilgrims. Not only does a pilgrimage performed in this way create community and a communal tradition, it also offers a public and performative Christian reaction to the difficulties regarding the church–state relations and the growing sensitivities about religious objects such as Islamic veils and headscarves, minarets and crosses in public or the growing presence of Islam in European society (cf. Grabow 2010: 94–95, 108). Boissevain has pointed out how the revival of rituals is linked to the coming of outsiders (1992: 9–16). This "answer" involves not only pilgrimages, but also includes a revaluation of other Christian rituals: in some countries the procession is back on stage as a renewed "contra-Reformational" instrument for the "invisible" Christian church and as an antidote to secularization and a growing public presence of Islam.[29] In that regard it is not irrelevant to mention that in Catholic tradition Saint James is the matamoros – the Moor-slayer – par excellence. In this way an informal mixed initiative of civil servants from the EU in Brussels and members of the Rocío Brotherhood for a Camino Europeo is also to be understood as a resacralization mission in the symbolic space called "Europe" (Plasquy 2010: 280–281).

Ill. 2: At the expo of Mini-Europe in Brussels the cathedral of Santiago de Compostela represents Saint James and the camino. The written explanation leaves nothing to the imagination: the Santiago pilgrimage devoted the Western world collectively to religion and also united the Christian world in its fight against the Moors. (Photo: Peter Jan Margry)

The idea of the new pilgrimaging along spiritual trails was a bottom-up movement, which was adopted later by the Church and European institutions. It is therefore not surprising that in 2004, in order to emphasize the importance of pilgrimages made on foot and the visitation of holy sites even more, under the collective auspices of the bishops' conferences in Europe, the Catholic Church organized an international pilgrimage to Santiago to mark the expansion of the EU with ten new member states. John Paul II used this occasion to once again hammer away at how the "soul of Europe rests on Christian values."[30] Moreover, according to him, Christianization had led to the unification of Europe which then, in 2004, was sealed on the economic and political level in the context of the EU. John Paul II was deeply sensitive to how, in the post-9/11 era, a moral, religious and cultural uncertainty had crept into Europe (cf. Drury 2004). Even in countries where secularism has to a certain extent become the norm, voices are beginning to be heard arguing that religion should again be allowed to play a larger role in politics and society. The argument is that mankind continues to have a need for religion, and that it still appears to be a stabilizing and civilizing factor. Pilgrimage in its elementary form, on foot, in reflection and silence, to the sacred sites that anchor Christianity geographically and spiritually, connects with the modern needs of the European citizen, offers space for ecumenical engagement and new forms of religiosity, puts Christianity forward again, and ultimately has salutary effects.

The cultural politics of European integration show a continuous interaction with the Christian roots of the subcontinent. With regard to the creation of a European identity, Chris Shore argues (2000: 231) that the European construction is the last and greatest of the Enlightenment grand narratives and that it instrumentalized its past for that purpose. Grace Davie pointed at the religious factor in the creation of a transnational European identity (Davie 2001). The paradox in the practice is however that all the while that the routes to Santiago were being employed from the top-down and being turned into a European trademark, at the same time a new narrative was being created that caught the popular imagination, realizing an informal bottom-up revaluation of Europe's Christian heritage which, as a form of transnational civil religion, transcends the nation-state and nationalism (cf. Warburg 2009).[31] The transnational is understood here as the public representation of a "European", Christian-based and inspired continent. The pilgrim roads have become a specific portmanteau construct in which contemporary European-wide needs for regained norms and values and new forms of religiosity and spirituality can be generated and provided with content. In their mediatized performance they form an overarching, binding factor in a morally and religiously divided European civil society that is seeking to find common bonds for its political and sociocultural unification and which matches with the secularized pluriform and individualized ways of religious consumption and infractions of other religions.

Civil Religion in Europe

Due to sociopolitical and religious changes in Europe, in the last two decades new varieties of religious practice and experience gained importance. This has been accompanied by the emergence of a religious-political problem related to the traditional religions which have been undermined. Where the traditional religions fail to create unity among groups whose values and lifestyles differ, the "quasi" or alternative religious expressions seem capable of achieving alternative forms of community. While civil religion theories are debated and reworked, no theoretical consensus has thus far been found, although the existence of particular forms of civil religion is usually acknowledged (Bellah 1974; Bellah & Hammond 1980; Coleman 1970; cf. Gehrig 1981). In light of this agreement, and on the basis of the analysis of two recent rituals of movement and contemplation – the silent march and pilgrim treks – I have sought to uncover new manifestations of civil religion and reveal their immanent power and transcendency.

On the one hand, the "Dutch" silent marches prove to be capable of realizing political-administrative changes and contributing to the solution of problems such as violence and insecurity, and on the other they locally fulfill an explicit coping function by which personal grief can be healed and processed, while at the same time ventilating feelings of anger and powerlessness. The "national" variant of the silent march also fulfills the latter function when, as an expression of civil religion, the march, with the aid of mediatized representations, exerts a similar unifying and therapeutic – comforting, exorcising – effect on the whole society. In this way the ritual is in concordance with civil religion's definition as a religious ritual and symbol system that relates the role of citizens and the position of society in space, time and history to people's conditions of ultimate existence and meaning.

The organization of the modern silent march manifests a high degree of active bottom-up involvement by citizens themselves. As a result of its mediatization the local march has become a widely known and accessible ritual. It can be characterized as part of the transcendent, universal religion of the nation that, from social-cultural and political contexts, assumes its shape in an implicit manner over Christian religion, an institutional religion that for its daily practice has been thoroughly relegated to the private sphere. The civil religion generated by the silent march – performed locally and mediatized nationally – embodies a consensus with regard to the wish and need for social cohesion, healing and recalibrated societal values that can manifest itself in a transcendent way in "an overarching sense of unity" for Dutch society.[32] The conclusion of some policy makers and researchers, that the silent march is a "ritual for the lack of anything better" (Jansen 2000), is thus unwarranted. The organization of the modern silent march is characterized by a great degree of active involvement by citizens themselves. As Bellah affirmed, "every community is based on a sense of the sacred and requires a context of higher meaning" (1974: 270); the silent marches connect sensitive questions around life and death and the norms and values of Dutch society with questions of morale and religious significance. Rooted in Dutch history, through time and its chain of memory, the silent procession has reinvented itself continuously and proved to be a qualitatively strong, expressive and effective ritual of wide appeal. At moments of collective trauma and emotional crisis this political and commemorative ritual, with a national base and the power to unite people, can generate a meaningful answer to events and feelings of unease that bring society and individual citizens into existential turmoil. Because of its widely accepted significance and its transcendent character, in secularized Dutch society silent marches can be considered as an expression of civil religion at a national level, in the way that Bellah has identified it, and in which I disagree with Philip Hammond, who finds civil religion only in an institutional context (Bellah & Hammond 1980: xiv, 41–42). The mobilizing agency of the marches fully underpins Cottle's theory on the mediatization of rituals in cases of societal and moral unrest.

While the Dutch example demonstrates that in direct relation to societal crisis and personal existential anxieties civil religion has become manifest, my second step was to deal with the question if civil religion can also be discerned on a European level in more or less related circumstances. In that case not only the heritage discourse of the *camino* and other pilgrims' trails is being enacted "from below", as a follow-up to the EU's heritage politics, which is to Schrire a search for a common ideal in the Christian pilgrimage tradition and heritage romanticism (Schrire 2006: 73–84), but so is the idea of Christian history and values. These aspects are expressed by an imagined community that has – as pilgrims or in any another respect – a specific relation to one of the many pilgrims' trails. They form a vehicle for the need for new forms of rituality, spirituality and religiosity in modern society. As argued above, this pursuit caused a crucial change in the pilgrimage, as the journey became an end in itself and the network of pilgrims' ways became more and more "decatholicized" and ecumenical, and functioned as an open spiritual domain for all Europeans. For many of those walking them, being in transit is a performative journey of purification and reassurance in which elements such as self-reflection, the experience of silence as an expression of the sacred, and a form given to Christian values are central. It does not matter that individual pilgrims have different motives or ideas; what counts in this respect is the mediatized concept of pilgrimage, to which Christian-inspired idiom and image already contribute unintentionally to going on the route. The mediatization of, and the cultural politics surrounding the pilgrims' ways have thus given "pilgrimage" a meaning beyond itself, which offers a moral and spiritual frame of reference for both European society as a whole, as it comes under increasing pressure and social disintegration, and for its citizens individually. This new pilgrims' praxis is an amalgam of symbols, myths and rituals within which, in the light of history and Christian heritage, the European citizen in modern European society can find support, both with existential problems and in the search for the meaning of life, which is in conformity with the interpretation of civil religion employed here. Although not a people's movement, it is a grassroots current and has a vanguard mobilization. For Europe as a whole this practice generates a stage for open spirituality and revitalizes Christian values and meanings, and works as a civil religion, as an aid in dealing with daily life problems and as an implicit counterweight against threatening influences of non-Christian religion and culture in Europe.

Both examples of mediatized rituals, if one would categorize them as such, are largely in line with Durkheim's idea of civil religion, as grassroots initiatives and expressions of deep values and collective sentiments of a notional community. They share the fundamental element of movement performed by individuals. They are expressions of movement meaningfully rooted in history as sacralizing ritual. Both practices have been stripped of certain divisive historical elements and connotations, being transformed into more neutral rituals that fit secular (or postsecular) Western society, but retain tradition (invented or otherwise) as a legitimizing factor. This creates an accessibility in which one can participate voluntarily and individually. Arising in societies under threat, both forms – one individual and one collective – in their mediatized form represent alternative public theologies centered around an ideal of a society at peace and possessing moral unity, which in both cases are reminiscent of the importance of the Christian tradition of which they are part. Especially after the turmoil of global terrorism and the subsequent, increasing laicization, society's need for civility has become stronger. Both rituals mirror problematic social and political relations in society. The imagined European and national communities seek cohesion, norms and values, and cultural canons and identity. These elements, related to present existential anxieties, can be found in these rituals, gaining through their mediatization a transcendental quality as civil religion.

Notes

1 Santiago puts civil religion and nationalism more or less on one line and concurs with Bryan Turner that the hypotheses on civil religion/nationalism are weak because of the "use of a methodology of analogy," which is neither developed nor tested empirically (2009: 400).

2 Thanks to Cristina Sanchèz-Carretero for her comments on an earlier version of this text, and to the anonymous reviewers of this journal.

3 The questionnaires make part of the project Processes of Heritagization along the Camiño of Santiago de Compostela: Route Branch Santiago-Fisterra-Muxia, a research project by the Institute of Heritage Sciences (Spanish National Research Council) in Santiago de Compostela, in collaboration with the Meertens Institute (Royal Netherlands Academy of Arts and Sciences) in Amsterdam.

4 The "conditions of ultimate existence and meaning" make these rituals differ from football fan behavior or other collective manifestations of a particular form of community that in a mediatized way is not able to generate a meaningful overarching unity as civil religion.

5 See for example the website http://partyflock.nl/topic/1080704:Stille_tocht_voor_Arenda_Klaassens.html with comments on the 2009 silent march for a traffic victim. Accessed March 31, 2011.

6 Cf. Willaime (1991) where he points to the possibility of the development of a civil religion for Europe.

7 For example, in the seventeenth and eighteenth centuries the Catholics in Amsterdam continued to walk the former route of the famous medieval procession of the Miracle of the Sacrament, "doing the procession" as it was then called. This was an individual, notional reproduction of the original procession. Inconspicuously, and indeed often in the evening or at night, Catholics walked the route of the procession in silent prayer.

8 Parsons (2002: 272) pointed at the capacity of civil religion in maintaining and adapting traditions to modernity.

9 The initial response to Duinmeijer's death was a one-off, municipality-sponsored demonstration march. Only later, in the 1990s – the time in which the silent march became the format for such cases in the Netherlands – a silent march characteristic of others from that period was again organized on a yearly basis to mark the date of his death.

10 Meanwhile, in 1996, neighboring country Belgium was confronted with the horrors in the Dutroux case. The popular anger on the situation sparked off mass "white" marches of a partly different character, as these marches primarily contested the corrupt and incompetent Belgian political and judicial establishment. Although the white march movement came to an end in 1998, since 2000 the "Dutch" silent march has come into use in Belgium as a "new" ritual mourning practice.

11 On the term in this context see Pouwels and Vegter (2002); also, it is argued that "senseless" violence or violence without a function or reason does not exist, cf. Blok (1991) and Vasterman (2001); for silent marches related to senseless violence, cf. Stengs (2007).

12 http://www.rtvoost.nl/nieuws/?nid=119519, 21 December 2010. Accessed March 31, 2011.

13 http://www.rtvoost.nl/nieuws/?nid=119519, posting by the parents and boyfriend of Nathalie, December 21, 2010. Accessed March 31, 2011.

14 Quotes from: http://www.nu.nl/algemeen/70690/venlo-loopt-massaal-mee-in-stille-tocht.html and http://www.rtvoost.nl/nieuws/?nid=119519. Accessed March 29, 2011.

15 http://www.condoleanceregister.com/index.php?page=register&id=2215&pagina=21, 6 September 2010. Accessed March 29, 2011.

16 See http://retro.nrc.nl/W2/Nieuws/1999/05/08/Vp/03.html. Accessed March 31, 2011.

17 http://www.rtvoost.nl/nieuws/default.aspx?nid=119519, December 21, 2010. Accessed March 31, 2011.

18 http://partyflock.nl/topic/1080704:Stille_tocht_voor_Arenda_Klaassens.html, December 9, 2009. Accessed March 31, 2011.

19 The phenomenon has spread internationally. Initially silent marches were occasional, like the silent march against poverty in London in 1996 or the silent marches by American groups against gun violence from 1996 on. Since 2000 the practice has been adopted in a more structural way in Belgium. Employees killed in the bombing of the UN headquarters in Baghdad were remembered in 2003 in New York; in 2004 a silent march was held in Birkenau in commemoration of the Holocaust. In 2005 the United World Federation raised the idea of organizing "Silent Marches for the Innocent Victims of War" all over the world. In 2009 35,000 people held a silent march in Hannover following the suicide of the depressed soccer goalie Robert Enke, and in 2010 5,000 participated in a silent march for the 21 Loveparade victims in Duisburg, Germany.

20 This interest arose first in France, where the major part of old trails and their Roman and Gothic cultural heritage are situated.

21 Meertens Institute, online questionnaire on the camino practice, informant no. 67.

22 www.katholieknederland.nl/soeterbeeck/archief/2007/detail_objectID611692.html. Accessed October 16, 2010.

23 Meertens Institute, online questionnaire on the camino practice, informants no. 7, 47, 71, 85.

24 Meertens Institute, online questionnaire on the camino practice, informants no. 59, 66.

25 Figures given by the Officina de Acogida al Peregrino in Santiago, including only pilgrims on foot or bicycle who traveled more than 100 kilometers. During Santiago's Holy Years peak numbers were counted: 154,613 in 1999, 179,944 in 2004 and 269,742 in 2010. When the numbers are related to the pilgrim's motives, spirituality is rising, while the cultural incentive seems to be going down. Of the pilgrims questioned in 1999, 75% had (or also had) a cultural motivation; in 2002 this was 34%. In 2002 66% had only a religious motivation (the figure for 1999 is not clear due to different phrasing and multiple answering possibilities) (Degen 2001: 50).

26 Meertens Institute, online questionnaire on the camino practice, informant no. 27.

27 An interesting example of this development is the renaming of one part of the German camino as an ecumenical pilgrims' way: "Ein Weg, der zu Fuß bereist wird, entwickelt sich zu einer Beziehungslinie: zwischen Ost und West, zwischen Jung und Alt, zwischen Christen und Nichtchristen" (transl.: "A way which is traveled by feet, develops into a relationship line between the East and the West, between the young and the old, between Christians and non-Christians"). Accessed on March 31, 2011 at: http://www.oekumenischer-pilgerweg.de/.

28 The Contemplation Path was created for religious denominations, followers of esoteric philosophies and even agnostics (Eberhart: 157–159).

29 In Dutch cities, for example, the Catholic Church organizes processions to make the Church more visible in the public realm and to keep up with the growing visible presence of the Islam.

30 "Pope stresses Christian values of enlarged EU," AFP, May 2, 2004, at: http://wwrn.org/articles/15346/?&place=eu§ion=christianity, accessed March 23, 2011.

31 Warburg (2009) also addresses the idea of the existence of transnational civil religion, as manifested in the celebration of America's national holiday (July 4) abroad, as performed by the transnational American community in Denmark.

32 The existence of a distinctive modern form of civil religion in the Netherlands was doubted earlier, see Laeyendecker (1986).

References

Albers, Ineke 2007: *Heilige kracht wordt door beweging losgemaakt: Over pelgrimage, lopen en genezing*. Groningen: Rijksuniversiteit Groningen.

Bal, Leon, Monique van Dijk-Groeneboer & Corja Menken-Bekius 2001: De stille tocht van Gorinchem: Een sociologische analyse. Praktische theologie. *Nederlands tijdschrift voor pastorale wetenschappen* 28, 278–291.

Barna, Gábor 2009: National Feasts, Political Memorial Rites – Feasts of Civil Religion? In: Ulrika Wolf-Knuts & Kathleen Grant (eds.), *Rethinking the Sacred*. Åbo: Åbo Akademi University, p. 101–110.

Bellah, Robert N. 1967: Civil Religion in America. *Daedalus* 96, 1–21.

Bellah, Robert N. 1974: American Civil Religion in the 1970's. In: Russel E. Richey & Donald G. Jones (ed.), *American Civil Religion*. San Francisco: Harper & Row.

Bellah, Robert N. & Philip E. Hammond 1980: *Varieties of Civil Religion*. San Francisco: Harper & Row.

Bijma, Berber 2007: *Herinnering aan alle zielen: Nieuwe rituelen om de doden te herdenken*. Zoetermeer: Meinema.

Bitton-Ashkelony, Brouria 2005: *Encountering the Sacred: The Debate on Christian Pilgrimage in Late Antiquity*. Berkeley: University of California Press.

Blok, Anton 1991: Zinloos en zinvol geweld. *Amsterdams Sociologisch Tijdschrift* 18, 189–207.

Boissevain, Jeremy (ed.) 1992: *Revitalizing European Rituals*. London: Routledge.

Caspers, Charles & Peter Jan Margry 2006: *Identiteit en spiritualiteit van de Amsterdamse Stille Omgang*. Hilversum: Verloren.

Christenson, James A. & Ronald C. Wimberley 1978: Who Is Civil Religious? *Sociological Analysis* 39, 77–83.

Coleman, John A. 1970: Civil Religion. *Sociological Analysis* 31, 67–77.

Coleman, Simon & John Eade (eds.) 2004: *Reframing Pilgrimage: Cultures in Motion*. London: Routledge.

Connerton, Paul 1989: *How Societies Remember*. Cambridge: CUP.

Cottle, Simon 2006: Mediatized Rituals: Beyond Manufacturing Consent. *Media, Culture & Society* 28:3, 411–432.

Cousineau, Phil 1998: *The Art of Pilgrimage: The Seeker's Guide to Making Travel Sacred*. Berkeley: Conari Press.

Davie, Grace 2001: Global Civil Religion: A European Perspective. *Sociology of Religion* 62:4, 455–473.

Degen, Horst 2001: Jakobuspilger – statistisch gesehen. *Die Kalebasse* 30 (July 2001), 48–50.

Döring, Alois (2003)2004: Auf Jakobs Wegen... Zur Erschließung der Jakobuspilgerwege im Rheinland und zur Aktualität der Pilgerreise. *Rheinisches Jahrbuch für Volkskunde* 35, 54.

Doss, Erika 2010: *Memorial Mania: Public Feeling in America*. Chicago: University of Chicago Press.

Drury, Shadia B. 2004: *Terror and Civilization: Christianity, Politics, and the Western Psyche*. New York: Palgrave Macmillan.

Durkheim, Émile (1912)2001: *The Elementary Forms of Religious Life*. Oxford: Oxford University Press.

Eberhart, Helmut 2006: Pilgrimage as an Example of "the past in the present". In: Fabio Mugnaini et al., *The Past in the Present: A Multidisciplinary Approach*. Catania: EdIt Press.

Everett, Holly 2002: *Roadside Crosses in Contemporary Memorial Culture*. Denton: University of North Texas Press.

Frey, Nancy L. 1998: *Pilgrim Stories on and off the Road to Santiago*. Berkeley: University of California Press.

Gamoran, Adam 1990: Civil Religion in American Schools. *Sociological Analysis* 51:3, 235–256.

Gehrig, Gail 1981: *American Civil Religion: An Assessment*. Norwich: SSSR.

George, Christian 2006: *Sacred Travels: Recovering the Ancient Practice of Pilgrimage*. Downers Grove: InterVarsity Press.

Grabow, Sven 2010: The Santiago de Compostela Pilgrim Routes: The Development of European Cultural Practice Policy and Practice from a Critical Perspective. *European Journal of Archeology* 13:1, 89–116.

Hervieu-Léger, Danièle 1999: *Le pèlerin et le converti: La religion en mouvement*. Paris: Flammarion.

Hervieu-Léger, Danièle 2000: *Religion as a Chain of Memory*. Cambridge: Polity Press.

Hjarvard, Stig 2008: The Mediatization of Religion: A Theory of the Media as Agents of Religious Change. *Northern Lights* 6, 9–26.

Hobsbawm, Eric 1983: Introduction: Inventing Traditions. In: Eric Hobsbawm & Terence Ranger (eds.), *The Invention of Tradition*. Cambridge: Cambridge University Press, pp. 1–14.

Hvithamar, Annika, Margit Warburg & Brian Arly Jacobsen (eds.) 2009: *Holy Nations and Global Identities, Civil Religion, Nationalism, and Globalisation*. Leiden: Brill.

Jansen, Jacques 2000: Stille Omgang: Een zoeken naar samenleving: Plechtigheden en morele verontwaardiging rondom "zinloos geweld". In: E. D'Hondt (ed.), *Zinloos geweld herdacht*. Baarn: Gooi & Sticht, pp. 65–79.

Kierkegaard, Søren (1844)1980: *The Concept of Anxiety: A Simple Psychologically Orienting Deliberation on the Dogmatic Issue of Hereditary Sin*. Reidar Thomte (transl.). Princeton, NJ: Princeton University Press.

Kim, Andrew E. 1993: The Absence of Pan-Canadian Civil Religion: Plurality, Duality and Conflict in Symbols of Canadian Culture. *Sociology of Religion* 54, 257–275.

Kleger, Heinz & Alois Müller (eds.) 1986: *Religion des Bürgers: Zivilreligion in Amerika und Europa*. München: C. Kaiser.

Kleger, Heinz & Alois Müller (eds.) 2004: *Religion des Bürgers: Zivilreligion in Amerika und Europa*. 2nd rev. ed. Münster: LIT.

Kötting, Bernard 1950: *Peregrinatio religiosa: Wallfahrten in der Antike und das Pilgerwesen in der alten Kirche*. Münster.

Laeyendecker, Leo 1986: Zivilreligion in den Niederlanden. In: Heinz Kleger & Alois Müller (eds.), *Religion des Bürgers: Zivilreligion in Amerika und Europa*, pp. 64–84.

Lane, Christel 1981: *The Rites of Rulers: Ritual in Industrial Society – the Soviet Case*. Cambridge: Cambridge University Press.

Lodewijkx, Hein F.M., Gaby L.E. Kersten & Martijn van Zomeren 2008: Dual Pathways to Engage in "Silent Marches" Against Violence: Moral Outrage, Moral Cleansing and Modes of Identification. *Journal of Community & Applied Social Psychology* 18, 153–167.

Lundby, Knut (ed.) 2009: *Mediatization, Concept, Changes, Consequences*. New York: Peter Lang.

Maclaine, Shirley 2000: *The Camino: A Journey of the Spirit*. New York: Simon and Schuster.

Margry, Peter Jan 2008a: Secular Pilgrimage: A Contradiction in Terms? In: Peter Jan Margry (ed.), *Shrines and Pilgrimage in the Modern World: New Itineraries into the Sacred*. Amsterdam: Amsterdam University Press, pp. 13–46.

Margry, Peter Jan 2008b: Stille tochten als *civil religion*. *Simulacrum, Tijdschrift voor kunst en cultuur* 17, 27–30.

Margry, Peter Jan & Cristina Sánchez-Carretero (eds.) 2011: *Grassroots Memorials: The Politics of Memorializing Traumatic Death*. New York: Berghahn.

Mathisen, James A. 1989: Twenty Years After Bellah: Whatever Happened to American Civil Religion. *Sociological Analysis* 50:2, 129–146.

Oursel, Raymond 1963: *Les pèlerins du moyen âge*. Paris: Fayard.

Parsons, Gerald 2002: *Perspectives on Civil Religion*. Aldershot: Ashgate.

Peelen, Janneke & Willy Jansen 2007: Emotive Movement on the Road to Santiago de Compostela. *Etnofoor* 20:1, 75–96.

Plasquy, Eddy 2010: El Camino Europeo del Rocío: A Pilgrimage towards Europe? *Journal of Religion in Europe* 3, 256–284.

Post, Paul, Jos Pieper & Marinus van Uden 1998: *The Modern Pilgrim: Multidisciplinary Explorations of Christian Pilgrimage*. Leuven: Peeters.

Post, Paul, Ronald L. Grimes, Albertina Nugteren, P. Pettersson & Hessel Zondag 2003: *Disaster Ritual: Explorations of an Emerging Ritual Repertoire*. Leuven: Peeters.

Pouwels, Nelly & Laura Vegter 2002: Meindert Tjoelker en de mythe van het zinloos geweld: Een exploratief onderzoek naar het verschijnsel "zinloos geweld". *Sociologische gids* 49, 9–25.

Povedák, István 2009: Hungarian Civil Religion and its Heroes. In: Ulrika Wolf-Knuts & Kathleen Grant (eds.), *Rethinking the Sacred*. Åbo: Åbo Akademi University, pp. 111–123.

Rowbottom, Anne 2001: Subject Positions: Monarchy, Civil Religion and Folk Religion in Britain. In: Gábor Barna (ed.), *Politics and Folk Religion*. Szeged: University of Szeged, pp. 137–152.

Rupp, Joyce 2005: *Walk in a Relaxed Way: Life Lessons from the Camino*. New York: Orbis.

Santiago, Jose 2009: From "Civil Religion" to Nationalism as the Religion of Modern Times: Rethinking a Complex Relationship. *Journal for the Scientific Study of Religion* 48:2, 394–401.

Schrire, Dani 2006: The Camino de Santiago: The Interplay of European Heritage and New Traditions. *Ethnologia Europaea* 36:2, 69–72.

Shore, Cris 2000: *Building Europe: The Cultural Politics of European Integration*. London: Routledge.

Stengs, Irene 2007: Commemorating Victims of "Senseless Violence": Negotiating Ethnic Inclusion and Exclusion. In: Peter Jan Margry & Herman Roodenburg (eds.), *Reframing Dutch Culture: Between Otherness and Authenticity*. Aldershot: Ashgate, pp. 159–179.

Van Dijk, Harmen 1999: Stille tocht na de dood van hond Boris. *Trouw*, 14 August.

Vasterman, Peter L.M. 2001: Zinloos geweld als mediahype: De aanjagende rol van de media bij de sociale constructie van zinloos geweld. *Tijdschrift voor Bestuurskunde* 10:7, 299–310.

Verbrugge, Ad 2004: *Tijd van onbehagen: Filosofische essays over een cultuur op drift*. Amsterdam: SUN.

Visser, Ellen 2002: In Venlo schreeuwen de zwijgenden het uit. *De Volkskrant*, 17 October.

Warburg, Margit 2009: Transnational Civil Religion: The Fourth of July in Denmark. In: Annika Hvithamar, Margit Warburg & Brian Arly Jacobsen (eds.), *Holy Nations and Global Identities, Civil Religion, Nationalism, and Globalisation*. Leiden: Brill, pp. 271–294.

Webb-Mitchell, Brett 2007: *School of the Pilgrim: An Alternative Path to Christian Growth*. Louisville: Westminster John Knox.

Willaime, Jean-Paul 1991: Les religions et l'unification européenne. Grace Davie & Danièle Hervieu-Léger (eds.), *Identités religieuses en Europe*. Paris: La Découverte.

Peter Jan Margry is an ethnologist. He studied history at the University of Amsterdam and holds a PhD from the University of Tilburg (2000). He is a senior research fellow at the Meertens Institute, a research center on culture and language of the Royal Netherlands Academy of Arts and Sciences in Amsterdam. His work focuses on contemporary religious culture, rituals, cultural memory and heritage. His last book is *Grassroots Memorials: The Politics of Memorializing Traumatic Death* (co-edited with Cristina Sánchez-Carretero, 2011, Berghahn).
(peterjan.margry@meertens.knaw.nl)

COLONIZING LATVIA?
A Piece of Swedishness in the Forests of Talsi

Mats Lindqvist

This article investigates the ways in which Latvian sawmill workers understand the effects of global capitalism in postsocialist Latvia, here represented by the establishment of a Swedish industry in the forest-rich region of Talsi. Technology, organization, language, culture, as well as "masters", are imported specially from Sweden, and all are deemed necessary in order to make the plant competitive. The article is concluded with a discussion of how we shall understand this kind of colonization project with stability as an inbuilt goal in relation to a world economy that all the more builds on transitory relationships to places, as well as rapid movements across state borders. The article also problematizes the conceptualizations of postsocialist studies in relation to concepts such as postcolonialism, neocolonialism and neocapitalism.

Keywords: workers culture, global capitalism, neoliberalism, neocolonialism, Latvia

In 2002, under the heading "Entrepreneurs in the world, not just in Sweden," the Swedish Trade Council described on their website the new global economic scene for Swedish entrepreneurs with ambitions to expand: "Now," it was claimed, "is a time of internationalization." The statement continued: "For you as an entrepreneur, this is a time of opportunities. Out there is now here at home. This provides you with new conditions to take your company where you want. (…) Now, it is markets and industries that decide, creating new business opportunities."[1]

Many companies have followed the rhetorical device that "out there is now here at home," such that the rhetoric is now borne out in reality. Thus in other information publicized by the Swedish Trade Council from the same year, exact records were issued about the expansion of Swedish companies on the other side of the Baltic Sea – such as in Latvia. In Latvia at this time there were 240 Swedish companies, altogether employing 10,385 people. While the majority was small-scale companies, employing between 10 and 20 people, larger companies, such as the clothing labels Almina and Anastasia, now based in Riga, employ 900 and 740 respectively. In addition, this region plays host to a number of smaller subsidiaries of well known Swedish corporations, such as ABB, Ericsson, Skanska and Electrolux.

These figures tell the tale of an expansive flow of capital, machine parks and entrepreneurs over the Baltic Sea since 1991, the year of Latvia's independence. One industry which, already early on in this process, was enticed by the hidden wealth in rural Latvia was the forest industry. The region of Talsi was particularly attractive in this respect, since 55 percent of the total area of the region was woodland. Bergkvist-Insjön – a sawmill plant with its head office in the province of Dalarna, Sweden – was one such company, which, as early as 1995, began to explore the possibilities for a sawmill plant in Lauciene, a village located about ten kilometres east of the city of Talsi.

In an autobiography, in a chapter entitled "Adventures in the East" (author's translation), one of the initiators, Ulf Bergkvist – the main owner and chairman of Bergkvist-Insjön – explains how it all began with a hunting trip to Estonia and Latvia in January 1993. Together with his sawmill colleague Karl Hedin and Lennart Daniels, an entrepreneur in the wood industry, Ulf was travelling on the forest roads hunting the skittish lynx (Bergkvist 2006). After a successful day for the band of would-be hunters, the organizer of the expedition, Daniels, exclaims: "Boys, this is precisely what I promised; an exciting lynx hunt in foreign lands. Furthermore, the outlays for this sort of expedition are, as you know, very low" (2006: 96).

The rendering the trip receives in Bergkvist's autobiographical account is clearly inscribed in a classic colonial discourse. We meet "civilized"[2] Europeans who during their hunting adventures in the Baltic "wilderness" not only encounter an excess of grouse, lynx and fox, but also human beings and countries in penury and deterioration, in need of Western solicitude, investment and expertise (cf. Domanski 2004). During the course of the journey the hunter's gaze is successively replaced with the gaze of the businessman, who begins to see slumbering pecuniary possibilities in the midst of post-Soviet disorder.[3] At the end of the chapter, Bergkvist summarizes his impressions thus:

> We had seen the vast, partly untouched and unkempt forest resources. In our eyes, they appeared underutilized, neglected, but just as well with a wood quality which in many respects is similar to Sweden.
>
> We had seen collapsed kolkhozy [a Russian form of collective farms] and old Soviet industry projects which were now left gray and deserted. (...) We had seen a whole lot of poverty, hardship and a population with a vast element of alcohol abuse. But we had also met hard-working and generous people with a strong belief in the future. (...) On our next trip, we were to penetrate deeper into the economic conditions surrounding forest values, local timber pricing, logging and shipping costs. (2006: 99)

The evaluation of these business opportunities was apparently successful; the building of the logging company Vika Wood would be initiated in 1995.[4] But the site was not new in all respects; the sawmill building in Talsi was bound up with the fate of another plant: the establishment of the Latvian site was causally connected to the closure of existing premises in Sweden. In a written history of the company, to be found on the website of the Upplandian[5] community Skyttorp, one could read:

> **Skyttorp's Saw and Carpentry Factory** (...) After the saw house had been burnt down on 1 March, 1987, a new and top modern sawmill was rebuilt on the same spot. After a new bankruptcy in 1991, the sawmill was bought by Domänverket in 1992, which subsequently sold it to Hebeda Trä [a company name, literally meaning 'Hebeda wood']. In the autumn of 1995 operations in the factory, which now has just over 20 people employed, will end, the sawmill will be dismantled and moved to Talsi, Latvia. The new name is Vika Wood.[6]

Swedish sawmill technology, in the form of complete facilities, coupled with the know-how of Swedish entrepreneurship migrated overseas, taking possession of what was considered virgin land. This transfer was preceded by market calculations and risk analyses about wood quality, infrastructure and wage costs. But, for the Swedish entrepreneur, one unknown quantity remained: the Latvian workforce. There may have been the acknowledgement that the Latvians are generous and hard-working; still, the entrepreneurs asked themselves: how will they adjust to new social and economic conditions, how will they manage the demands of a modern, capitalist industry, especially after decades of a communist-planned economy?

Background, Aim and Methodology

This specific case study is part of a larger everyday- and actor-oriented research project, which has as its primary focus transnational movements of capital, factories, commodity, services and workforce in the Baltic Sea area.[7] Throughout this research process, I have investigated the ways in which, in different local and national contexts, industry workers both understand and cope with the new work-related conditions that have been instigated by processes of Europeanization and globalization, processes which, while doubtlessly economic, must be viewed in light of the development of new information and communication technology, and, politically, against the backdrop of the ideological hegemonization of neoliberalism (Castells 1996; Harvey 2005).

In a newly completed study, I discuss the personal accounts of vulnerability and insecurity, as they come to be experienced by the employees of Flextronics – a transnational corporation, which has manufacturing facilities in the Swedish towns of both Karlskrona and Visby (Lindqvist & Lindqvist 2008). Threats of relocation are ever present, sometimes drastically concretized by the wholesale closure of factories. It is a fate which, with the advent of the new millennium, was inflicted upon Flextronics in Visby. There, the workforce saw "their" production distributed to other branches within the corporation, but also to the national competitor in Karlskrona, as well as Gdansk in Poland, and to one of the corporation's Hungarian facilities. It is for comparative purposes that the Flextronics study will be combined with the case of the sawmill in Talsi.

The aim of the present article is to critically assess the ways in which the effects of global capitalism in postsocialist Latvia are discussed and interpreted in the context of a Swedish sawmill company that uprooted and relocated to the forest-rich region of Talsi. The key question is, what is the character of such a project when viewed and evaluated from societal contexts with different historical, political and cultural conditions? What do these historical experiences mean for the employees' ways of understanding the influx of foreign capital and Western knowledge, when the border opens towards a world outside of the Eastern bloc? Concomitantly, how do the Swedish entrepreneurs view both the investment and the Latvian workforce recruited for the purposes of production? To what extent is this foreign investment to be seen as some kind of neocolonialism[8]?

Methodologically, the study belongs to the ethnographic tradition. The approach is qualitative, and the analysis is based on a number of narratives, all of which articulate the same phenomenon from different positions. The material from which this study draws consists of fifteen interviews, all with employees at Vika Wood, and all collected between the years of 2004 and 2005. The sample is not systematic; instead it consists of people in the areas of both production and management who on request were willing to participate in the study. The composition of informants is mixed. It includes both men and women of different ages, and all are ethnic Latvians. The interviews were conducted in Latvian and translated into Swedish. The length of the conversations – which took place in the workplace, cafés, or in the workers' homes – varied between one and three hours. The quotes taken from the interviews, and which are used in this text, serve as examples so as to give an impression of some of the more dominant trends emerging out of the interview material. For reasons of limited space, the article does not allow particular attention to be paid to any specific variations within these broader trends. The analysis is also based on a longer interview with the Swedish CEO (conducted in March 2010), as well as other sources, including the CEO's autobiography (published in 2006) and related narratives, as told through newspaper articles, relevant websites and other Internet data.

Postsocialism and Global Capitalism

This study can be positioned in the anthropological field of research that seeks to interrogate the effects of global capitalism on local class relations and the life situation of individuals (cf. Miller 1997;

Ong 1987, 2006; Rothstein & Blim 1992; Mandel & Humphrey 2002). Sharryn Kasmir summarizes this in a short and concise manner: "anthropologists document what global capitalism looks like when it 'lands'" (1999).

Considering the geographical and political context, this ethnographic research can also be placed within the broad field of postsocialist studies. This field of scholarship acknowledges the necessity of understanding overarching theories about "the transition" in relation to the social practices and constructions of meaning of everyday life (cf. Burawoy &Verdery 1999; Hann 2002). On the quotidian level, "the transition" is rarely a simple and one-dimensional path from one economic-political system to another. When a study takes its starting point at the locus of single places and individuals it soon becomes clear that there are radically different ways in which postsocialist change is lived, experienced and interpreted. The strength of this perspective is that it shows how specific places, depending on their local history, follow different paths in the way of approaching and dealing with this profound transformation. The multiplicity of specific conditions function as tools to articulate contemporary everyday practices, in a situation of uncertainty, where the past is interwoven with the future (Kalb 2002: 323). The transformation never entails a simple break with the past, nor is it the case that the future is eminently predictable (Hörschelmann & Stenning 2008: 345).

In parallel with this broad research, a rather animated debate has ensued over whether the concept of *postsocialism* is a suitable umbrella term for studies conducted within the Eastern bloc. David A. Kideckel has remarked that it is a peculiar term, since it defines societies as what they are not, rather than what they are (2002: 115) – a discussion to which I wish to return at the end of the article. Another problem is that the concept of postsocialism homogenizes an expansive area of land that in reality is heterogeneous in relation to the differing developmental paths that each state has taken, a relationship that not least anthropological studies have been able to confirm. It has also been pointed out that terms like *socialism* and *postsocialism* easily lead to a kind of geographic, ethnographic and methodological isolationism (cf. Owczarzak 2009: 3). Boundaries that can prevent a broader understanding of the processes taking place in this part of the world are created.[9] In this context, one can regard the dichotomy of East and West as convenient shorthand, left over from the days of the Cold War, one that is still central to how academic studies on societal transformation are both organized and understood. One effect of this discourse is that the talk of "societal transformation" refers to the East, while simultaneously the West is assigned the function of both, descriptively, the economic and political model and, normatively, the role model to which the East is compared and contrasted, and ultimately forced to conform. The relationship implies a hierarchization based on a difference in time and space; West represents the advance with which East has to play catch up (Hörschelmann 2002).

Katherine Verdery designates a way beyond this trope of in-contemporaneity, and in a way that transgresses the divide between the East and West. The point of departure for this perspective is her discussions concerning the possibility of applying postcolonial studies to the postsocialist context (1996, 2002). Analogous to the discussion on Orientalism – which Edward Said famously articulated – the East functions as the "Other" of the West. Thus, it is not just the colonies of the Third World but also socialism in the Second World that function as the constitutive outside in the construction of the "Western" (cf. Owczarzak 2009: 5). Verdery states that both postsocialism and postcolonialism have their foundation in the same historical time, that of the Cold War (2002: 18).[10]

Therefore, she proposes "post-Cold-War studies" as a term that links seemingly disparate regions like Africa and Eastern Europe in an analysis of the process of global capitalism. Moreover, and inspired here by postcolonial theory, Verdery makes a swift and meaningful turn by stating that the Cold War is not over; there is still reason to divide the world in a "West" and the "Rest", which in the case of postsocialist studies discloses itself through an investigation into the transfer of Western institutions and know-how to the states of the former Eastern Bloc, a kind of research that enriches the general knowledge of neocolonial processes (2002: 19). Don Kalb assents to this description, adding that the Cold War has only changed character. Gone is the obsession with conventional territorial conquest and border control. Such strategies have been replaced with more sophisticated forms of institutional and cultural warfare (2002: 324). Nina Glick Schiller sees in finance capitalism such a neocolonial form that gives dominant states power over others, without recourse to any military occupation or direct colonization. Rather, neocolonial strategies often appear in supposedly humanitarian and altruistic forms such as loans, investments and aid activities (cf. Hassler 2003: 191). According to Glick Schiller, it is important to reintroduce a discussion of politics and power inequalities between states into the field of transnational studies and globalization (2006: 9–10).

So as to reconnect these general thoughts back to the present study, the thoughts of Verdery, Kalb, Glick Schiller, amongst others, should serve as a warning to us, namely that such attention to cultural, social and historical specificity, should not obscure certain similarities between general tendencies of neocolonialism in operation in the present conjuncture and, for our purposes, the relation that exists between Sweden and Latvia. As a consequence of the end of the Cold War and the entry of postcommunist states into the European Union – as well as the international trade of capital and commodities – countries like Sweden and Latvia are today subjected to similar forces in relation to economic globalization. Up until the financial crisis in 2009, Latvia constituted an attractive country for foreign investment. The speed of reform in a neoliberal direction was notable, also within a global comparative framework. In 2005, under the euphemistically edged criterion of "ease-of-doing-business", the World Bank ranked the Latvian state in 26th place (of 150) (Woolfson 2008: 80).[11]

Other similarities hold, however. Both countries are currently located in a political, economic and cultural hinterland, caught within the indeterminate time of the "post-". *After* strong national borders and strict state control of the economy – which is to say, in the case of Sweden, *after* the golden age of the welfare state and, in the case of Latvia, *after* the Soviet communist regime. The effects of postsocialism on Sweden are clear, none more so than in terms of its ideological drift; the socialist line, which, for so long, the Swedish social democrats tacked, lost both direction and momentum in the 1980s, during which time neoliberal ideas began to gain ground within the movement (cf. Harvey 2007: 23). This neoliberal advance in the West, later conjoined with the postcommunist era in Eastern Europe, has contributed to its vicelike hegemonic grip, strangling all political alternatives (socialism or any other economic model) as live possibilities.

The Good Father

A palpable difference between the Swedish electrical fitters employed by Flextronics and Latvian sawmill workers at Vika Wood is that the latter express very few complaints about the course development has taken after national independence and Latvia's subsequent economic integration as a free market economy. They claim to be pleased with the working environment, the management, wages, colleagues etc. – with life in general. They regard themselves as subordinates in what is otherwise a positive cumulative process, in which everything is always-already improving – a common trope which hearkens back to the modernist narrative of progress. What gives these workers a sense of security and belief in the future is, however, neither the significance of Latvia's regained independence, nor the fact that, since 2004, the country has been a member of the European Union. Most of them may have voted for EU membership, but mainly because they felt there was no alternative. When the topic is broached in conversation, concern is raised about the dangers of being swallowed up by a new empire, so soon after the gaining of national political independence. When, on the other hand, they speak in favour of EU integration, the justification is couched in terms of national security, namely protection from the perceived threat coming from its neighbour in the East (jfr Herd & Löfgren 2001).

If it is neither a pride in national sovereignty nor unity in an integrated Europe that explains the sense of confidence experienced amongst Latvian workers, then it is because this confidence has another source: the newly established, foreign-owned companies that have taken root there since Latvia opened its borders to Europe and the Western world. One of them is Vika Wood, of which 60 percent was owned by Swedish capital interests, with the remaining 40 percent belonging to the Finnish trading house Thomesto (Bergkvist 2006: 103). The Swedish ownership was particularly active, because the operations in Lauciene were to a great extent directed from its parent company in Insjön, Sweden.

Ivars Grintals, who works at Vika Wood, gives voice to a general attitude about the company, when he remarks:

> the best wages in all of Kurland, you have at Vika. The best workplace – nothing like it exists elsewhere. If Vika Wood did not exist, I would still have worked in the slaughter house.

Vika Wood is the type of company that emerged as a direct consequence of economic globalization – of free trade and open borders, a free market economy which seems to have taken over from the Soviet state like a kind of people's protector, a guardian of the people.[12] The new Latvian state has, in accordance with neoliberal overtures, prescribed that politics be divorced from economics, and that politics have a more obscure role in the daily life of its citizens. In such an ideological climate, the political task of the state is restricted to ensure that the private right to ownership, the free market and free trade is guaranteed (Harvey 2005: 2), which paradoxically demonstrates that, in practice, the market economy cannot work without political intervention (Venn 2009: 212). There is then, even if exponents of neoliberalism would disavow it, an intimate relation between individual sovereignty and legislative authority which carries on unabated in the transition from the Soviet model to the present consolidation of a market-based democracy.

But let us move away from a principled likeness to an evaluation of the two alternatives. When one listens to the narratives of the sawmill workers about the many advantages of Vika Wood, one gets the impression that a "bad" patriarch has left the room, only to be replaced with a "good" one. To speak with Katherine Verdery, one could say that "socialist paternalism" (1993: 39) has simply been replaced with a neocapitalist one.[13] All companies are of course not of the exemplary kind. On the contrary, there are quite a few "bad fathers" left in the region; for example in the form of the slaughter house, of which Grintals reminds us in the aforementioned quote. A telling fact is that the foreign-owned companies appear to have immunity from such characterizations. Indeed, very often the working conditions experienced during the Soviet era are used as a convenient foil with which to contrast the "new" and "ideal" conditions described. Such is the case with Grintals when he recollects:

> In those days there were kolkhozy, they just shouted at you, pressured you, always. But here there is no boss shouting at you. You do your job and everything is perfect … I cannot find words to describe our management … if you so woke me up in the middle of the night, I would say that it is the best management you can get.

Grintals' recollection plays on classical patriarchal relationships. First, the cruel master is described as the one who (through his intermediary) barks orders at his subjects; thereafter the benign master is installed, reigning with a gentle hand. Here also are exhibited the typical elements of deference and humility.

The Swedish Model

The Swedish-owned company appears to have found loyalty, order and discipline from the employees on a mode of thinking which builds on friendliness, honesty and care. By examining the details as to how specifically the working conditions are organized at Vika Wood (both inside and outside of the workplace), it is possible to see an attempt by the owners to implement parts of what is often referred to as "the Swedish model".[14] *In nuce*, such a model builds on a will to compromise, on a peaceful coexistence between both parties of the employer–employee relation. It carries with it an idea that only social welfare can guarantee high productivity which will be of mutual advantage for work and capital, for worker and capitalist alike. At bottom, there is an investment in an idea of shared social responsibility (see Hort 1994). This is teeming with cultural significance. At stake is an attempt to form and shape the Latvian workforce in accordance with Swedish norms, habits and recommendations, adjudged to be conducive to high productivity. The region is thus not merely penetrated economically, but culturally.

We get a better picture of this process if we study the Vika Wood's website. It says the company's goal is to produce sawn goods of Scandinavian standard (which implies high standard, indirectly inferring that the Latvian standard is of lesser quality). With regards to drying, measurements and shipment we are informed that "this will be accomplished through experience and knowledge from Swedish owned sawmills to the local work force, both blue and white."[15] Under the heading "History" one can further read that this transfer of Swedish technology and knowledge already began two years before the production started in 1997. The building may have commenced in 1995 and continued in 1996. But the actual construction of the site was, at the same time, combined with "training people in the parent company in Sweden."[16]

It was not considered possible to induct the would-be Latvian workforce in Talsi into new employment practices. The presumptive employees were initially recruited through a rigorous selection process, which, according to information from the Swedish owner, was intended first and foremost to weed out the ones adjudged to be suffering from alcohol problems. Here we encounter a common part of a Western colonial discourse, namely the portrayal of the "Others" in the East as bearers of bad habits, idleness and lack of self-discipline (Buchowski 2006). Those who passed the test were sent to the parent company in Sweden, located next to the river Dalälven in the village of Insjön. But the intention was wider than merely a conveyance of the requisite technological skills needed for modern timber production at Bergkvist-Insjön. The 35 selected (more or less) workers were placed in separate houses and flats in the village, with the expectation that they would live and partake in community life for about a year. In these surroundings, the Latvian workers would acquire a proficiency in Swedish; this they would achieve through socializing with the locals. But, also, through being encouraged to participate as an active member of the community – like for example the celebration of Midsummer and rowing contests on Dalälven – it was hoped that the Latvian workers would imbue and live their lives through Swedish cultural practices. It was no longer sufficient to show competence qua sawmill worker; rather, the model of the ideal worker in this case was constituted through a set of ethnic attributes and socially embedded practices. By speaking Swedish, by thinking and practising "Swedishness", but moreover by taking heed of the advice proffered by his "Swedish" counterpart, in order to internalize his working practices to the highest possible degree – it was argued that, on these bases, the project on the other side of the Baltic Sea would have an improved chance of profitability. By internalizing a "Swedish" work ethic – in terms of professional integrity and other everyday behaviour – the Latvian workers were expected to become culturally competent as producers in a capitalist economy. Daphne Berdahl writes in a similar vein about the experiences of Eastern Germans who, after the integration into the united Germany, were imagined to suffer from a lack of cultural competence as consumers in a market economy, and which therefore called for intense "enlightening" activities (2005).

However, education in the Swedish language was not just to be carried out in Insjön. In the town of Talsi, and the village Lauciene also, courses were arranged for parts of the local population, not directly engaged in the activities at Vika Wood. This meant a significant part of people living in the region being conversant, to a greater and lesser degree, in Swedish. This active construction (this "Swedish-making") extended, then, far beyond the bounds of the immediate and proximal needs of the company.

The production manager at Vika Wood speaks excellent Swedish, not least because he must liaise with his Swedish superior on the phone several times a day. During these phone calls, the problems that invariably stem the flow of production are discussed. This indelible presence of "Swedishness" in Vika Wood's daily activities is further compounded by the fact that a Swedish contact is a frequent guest at the sawmill. Therefore, while the day-to-day management is left to the Latvian workforce, this is only nominally the case; rather, an atmosphere of constant monitoring shows up the ever-presence of Swedish expertise, even when physically absent. In this way, the geographical distance between the headquarters in Sweden and the subsidiary in Latvia is bridged. Swedish dominance, in the form of ownership and leadership (and a presumably higher knowledge capital), is thereby ensured, consistently redrawn and reiterated via representative contact and scrupulous monitoring.

But the Latvian workers are the first to draw out the positives. For them, this cultural presence shows itself not as needless meddling but as a sign of a sincere interest in the well-being of its employees. After all, the owners pay relatively high wages, social security contributions and see to it that the state cash in the regulated taxes. The interviewees were thus of the persuasion that this kind of felicitous behaviour towards both employees and the state was an exception and not the rule. As Girts Kierpe says:

> This company gives us more than what the state gives. We have a card, which means that the company has insured us. If you need, for example, a quick surgical treatment you can use this card ...

Another interesting imprint of the symbolic significance of "Swedishness" derives from the name given to the Latvian sawmill. "Vika" in Vika Wood is the name of a small village in the middle of Dalarna. Similar to the previously mentioned Skyttorps Sågverk (Skyttorp's Sawmill), and Toftans Sågverk, Vika Vimo Sågverk belonged to one of the three industries bought up and closed down in accord with the business plan that made possible the financing of the company's relocation to Latvia (Bergkvist 2006: 103). The name of Vika followed the new subsidiary as a reminder of its national and regional origins. Since Dalarna is often characterized as the most genuine Swedish province in the kingdom, the choice of name is laden with particularly strong national connotations. The name operates as a signifier which marks the land[17] and buildings as being the propriety of Sweden (Frykman & Löfgren 1987). This might seem obvious; nonetheless, it is still worth noting that the naming was a particular concern for the foreign owners, a matter over which the population of Talsi did not exercise any influence.

No Union, Please

The strong union tradition – arguably a central element in the Swedish model – has been entirely absent in the cultural transmission process at Vika Wood. Trade unionism has undoubtedly buttressed a strong social democratic heritage, playing a formative role in the shaping of the identity of modern Sweden.[18] Even if the impact of the unions has decreased over the last decades (an attrition resulting from increased individualization, privatization, flexibility and decentralization), the prevailing norm is still that each wage worker is a member or should hold union membership (Sverke & Hellgren 2002). While the union movement in Sweden has lost members in recent restructurings of its economy, Sweden's level of organization remains comparatively high (Andersen 2006; Kjellberg 2009).

Here, though, a certain limit is reached as to how far entrepreneurs are willing to transpose the Swedish model onto their foreign investments. The sawmill workers at Vika Wood are surprised, not to say slightly shocked, when asked about the absence of union recognition in their workplace. They readily seek to reassure how they have everything they could possibly need; why, they say, "rock the boat" by broaching such a demand with their benign employers? It is clear that on their visits to Sweden – where they were schooled in the skills of the trade by Swedish colleagues – no thoughts were given with respect to the long-standing relations between unions and companies in Swedish society. Whether the reason was due to a relatively low level of union consciousness among the employees at Insjön, or, alternatively, if the local union deliberately avoided any form of engagement, it would be improper to conjecture. All in all, not many references were made to the Swedish workers who acted as supervisors during their time at Insjön. Nor, for that matter, were the workers forthcoming when it came to talking about their social involvement in the village.

It is obvious that the actor steering the process of establishing a Swedish industrial project in the woods of Talsi is the band of entrepreneurs, investors and company leaders. Only this side of the two dominating parties within the Swedish job market has had direct influence over the regulations and principles upon which relations between employer and employees at Vika Wood have been founded. In Sweden, due to a strong, collectively mobilized counterforce, employers were often pushed into a politics of compromise. However, this was not the case in Latvia. Such a situation afforded businesses the opportunity to create a little home out-there, on foreign shores – at least, as the party of the employer would have us see it – all the while sifting through the traditions and practices of Sweden that did not altogether fit with their neoliberal worldview. One could say that the work practices installed at Vika Wood were predicated on a neoliberal utopia, namely a society based on free entrepreneurship with minimal political intervention. It was an ideal that could find its realization only outside of the borders of Sweden; indeed, as the research of the sociologist Charles Woolfson testifies, Latvia soon became the ideal country in this respect (Woolfson 2008).

The unions, that other potent actor in Swedish political and economic life, have not taken any active part in this adventure of colonization. Judging from what has taken place historically, it seems as though the political obligation of the enshrinement of workers' rights have to a greater extent coincided with the borders of the nation state.[19] Seemingly the right of economic migrancy has its limits, after all. When the borders towards the East opened, the economic elite may have seen business opportunities flourish. But, for the unions it has mostly entailed a threat to the livelihood of its members. Economic globalization carries the real risk that the strong gains made by the Swedish workers movement during the twentieth century in securing advantageous working conditions might be unceremoniously rolled back. Founded on my own study about Flextronics workers in Sweden, workers' concerns about the opening towards the East often return to an anxiety about wage dumping and unemployment (Lindqvist & Lindqvist 2008; Lindqvist 2010). An illuminating example in this regard, which coveted much attention internationally, was the so-called "Vaxholm conflict". Here, a Latvian building company responsible for building a school in Vaxholm, a city in Sweden, was said to pay substantially lower salaries to its Latvian workforce than the negotiated minimum wages secured for Swedish builders (Woolfson & Sommers 2006; Picard 2008).

But even if the union movement had taken a more active part in the establishment of this Swedish-owned company in Latvia, by applying more pressure for union recognition, the successes of such an intervention are far from guaranteed. One cannot underestimate the prevailing paternalistic attitudes harboured by many of the Latvian sawmill workers. In interviews, it becomes obvious that they do not associate unions as a natural element in market-economic relations. As has been illustrated by a great deal of research in the area, the union is rather an institution associated with the communist-planned economy and, by implication, is articulated with the oppression of the Soviet era (see Kubicek 2004; Bohle 2006; Ost 2009).

It is in this context that we can introduce a movement tending in the opposite direction to capital flows and investment paths. Such a movement does not concern capital and machines, but the free movement of people. We are introduced to the economic migrant, who, as a consequence of unemployment and hardship in the home country, offers his or her services for relatively low prices in Western countries such as Sweden (cf. Eglitis & Lace 2009). Such is the case with the Vaxholm example cited above. The corollary is that the denomination of "low costs", about which entrepreneurs and investors enthuse as the capital advantage of placing production in the Baltic States, has begun to gain currency within Swedish businesses.

The Gathering Clouds

Even if the sawmill workers at Vika Wood claim to be very pleased with the working conditions within the foreign-owned company,[20] they are, at the same time, not unconscious of the fact that Europeanization and economic globalization have their less salubrious effects. One can catch a glimpse of such reticence and resistances in conversations. There are also signs and events in geographically neighbouring regions, showing that the conditions for business and work in the Baltic States are not too dissimilar to Sweden. Robert Matisons, who is also employed at Vika Wood, explains how there is currently a shortage of wood, which means that there are fewer working hours than usual at the plant. In his words:

> There has been talk about importing wood from Belarus, but no wood arrives. There are a few sawmills that have moved to Belarus since the government of Belarus does not allow wood to be exported out of the country. Then they moved the production to Belarus – companies which have the same type of production as Vika Wood...

Matisons realizes that the destiny of other sawmill workers in Latvia could also affect him. "The move of production" is a phenomenon of intimidation equally true here as it is for the Swedish electrical fitters working at Flextronics – a company which lacks a home country and thus has no duties towards any locality where it sets up its site for commerce. Matisons' hopes for the future is that Vika Wood shall stay in the country until he himself retires, an event scheduled in ten years. It is noteworthy that he speaks of ten years. The board chairman, Ulf Bergkvist, says in an interview for the Swedish local paper *Dalademokraten* in 2004 (April 13) that the investments in the Baltic states are presently very profitable and that he expects the good times to last for a further ten to fifteen years. In that statement one can forebode that the Bergkvist-Insjön's possession of Talsi is seen as temporary, interesting only for as long as the venture is "profitable".

But the threat to (relative) welfare does not come from the volatility of foreign capital. The logic of the game of the market is to be followed, not questioned. The strangers who are feared and blamed are rather workers from abroad who are prepared to sell their labour-power for a lower price than the Latvians will accept. Robert Matisons speaks of those who always intrude "us Latvians", at the present not the Russian masters, but now, as a consequence of globalization and European integration, people who are festooned with the label "economic refugees". Turks are mentioned as an example, with the addition: *They come here and want to work at Vika Wood and they do it cheaper.*

This talk is pretty remarkable, since the interviewer also hears the views of many Latvians who now work abroad, both inside and outside of the European Union, for example in Norway, Ireland, Germany, Sweden, Hungary et cetera. As the case of the conflict in Vaxholm shows, the Eastern European workforce is attractive on the Western European job market, since they usually work for lower wages compared to the domestic workforce. But such cases are not spoken of as "economic refugees" – even if it would be justifiable to say so, considering the problems of unemployment and poverty with which Latvia is presently struggling (cf. Eglitis & Lace 2009). So, the motif for this migration to "abroad" is similar to the wishes of the workers in the Talsi region to gain employment in the foreign-owned Vika Wood. In this connection, one can possibly speak of an inner and an outer migration with the common aim, via abroad, to reach welfare and security in a working situation which is equivalent to the one the workers think exists in the West.[21]

In this view of economic migrants, there is, across the Baltic Sea, agreement. Workers on both sides relate to the same discourse on the relationship between national territory and "refugees". It appears as if the volatility of capital and work becomes visible and possible to question only when it takes the form of the "foreign worker". This attitude relates to a customary strand of thought within the workers movement, namely to perceive "outsiders" as potential threats, as with "strike breakers", in the initial stage of a strike (Pajares 2008).

Conclusion

As previously mentioned it was half a decade since I undertook the fieldwork for this study. Considering the rapidity of movement and rearrangements of capital and machine parks in the global order, which David Harvey has called the order of "flexible accumulation" (1989), it is fair to presume that many significant events, directly or indirectly impacting on Vika Wood, have taken place. As I mentioned earlier, Ulf Bergkvist's more or less explicit intention was for the Swedish engagement with Vika Wood to endure for a further ten to fifteen years. But interest cooled far earlier. Already three years subsequently, the Swedish capital stakeholders had left Vika Wood.[22] The reason, published in *Falu Kuriren* in 2006 (September 21), was indicated by Bergkvist as part of a new "business strategy". Henceforth, the company would concentrate its efforts on the home market. That, in reality, the reason was limited to issues of profitability does not appear likely, considering what is declared in the historiographic note on its website about the good and positive ways in which the company has developed.

The prompt decampment from Talsi was not particularly surprising considering the rapid mobility which generally prevails on the transnational finance and business markets. A company that fits well into that turbulence is the telecom corporation Flextronics, which I have investigated in a parallel study. Flextronics does not have a home country. It moves from place to place over the world; the choice of location for manufacturing is solely steered by questions of profitability. If it is considered advantageous for the company as a whole, facilities can swiftly be liquidated and new ones erected in presently more lucrative locations (Lindqvist & Lindqvist 2008).

But in the example regarding the Swedish-owned Vika Wood in Latvia there is something which appears irrational from a strictly profit-maximizing perspective, particularly when one considers that the activities were divested when the sawmill had advanced to be the largest one in Latvia.[23] If flexibility, risk management, and the importance of avoiding territorial duties are the watchwords within late modern transboundary capitalism, then why this drive to possess Latvian ground and Latvian minds? Why such an emphasis on draping the project in "Swedishness"? Why establish such strong, emotional ties between Swedes and Latvians, through, amongst other things, a year-long stay for the prospective workforce in the village of the Swedish headquarters?

There is a difference between Flextronics and Bergkvist-Insjön to which one must pay attention. In the first case, we are dealing with a transnational corporation which lacks territorial anchorage,[24] while in the latter case we are dealing with a relatively small company with a clear regional and national residence. The conditions for transnational industry establishments differ by the way in which the latter company's establishment of Vika Wood in Latvia is seen as a national extension of a mother activity with a solid national anchorage. The sawmill on the other side of the Baltic Sea can, for that reason, be regarded as an economic supplement to an activity which is perceived as Swedish – regardless of which national soil may serve these genuine Swedish business interests. The Swedish-making-process is, from that perspective, an unreflected way of legitimating this circumstance.

Another possible explanation has its ground in the specific societal context in which the establishing takes place. In brief, such an explanation would amount to emphasizing the strength which the construction of sameness demands in a reality which until recently has been deeply penetrated by a political and economical system that demands the maintenance of another type of subject. So, at the same time as the Latvians were conceived as ideal for a market-economy production by not being union organized, culturally they were perceived as not yet properly equipped for functioning effectively in a profit maximizing organization. The Swedish-making was, from this vantage point, a way of transferring individuals who were socialized in a planned economic system over to a mentality, a life style and a work ethic that was presumed to make, in a climate of global competition, Vika Wood a successful company. Thus a colonial discourse intersected with nationalism, since parts of the Swedish model and everyday culture were utilized as an instrument for first deculturation, then neoliberal acculturation.

Neocolonialism is a suitable concept to describe transnational processes of this kind. It is a type of colonialism that is more difficult to distinguish than its classic counterpart, since it, as previously mentioned, occurs with neither elements of violence nor any clear state intervention. "The transition" is, in this regard, seen as the path to "normalization". David Kideckel is, as I previously mentioned, critical against the concept of postsocialism, since it obscures what this normalization process is really about, namely an unreflexive attitude towards a specific form of capitalism. He means that the problem is not that the development is too slow, but too fast; not too little capitalism but too much. Neocapitalism is Kideckel's term for this variant, and which, with regards to social inequalities and class differences, far exceeds its Euro-American form (2002: 115). Without a strong middle-class and any durable democratic traditions, the gap between elite and underclass is extensive. One can assume that such a variant generates different forms of resistance than those we find in Western societies. To use Karl Polanyi's model, the East is (still) missing the double movement, that is, a strongly organized societal defence, so as to counteract the negative effects of a self-regulated capitalism ([1994]2002: 155ff.). The form of capitalism that people in the former Eastern Bloc were confronted with in the early 1990s was not perceived as a neoliberal modification, but capitalism per se. There was, therefore, and "ideally speaking", no room for any form of political regulation. A strong individualism was coupled with an equally strong anticollectivist trend. Against that background, it is not difficult to understand the lukewarm reception to unions that appears in the interview material. It is not a matter of lacking enlightenment from the West, but more about the prevailing circumstances that seem not to make possible countermovements that one would often associate with forms of resistance in the West. The sawmill workers' general talk of the working conditions at Vika Wood shall therefore not be understood as a sign of neither complacency nor ignorance, but as a rather logical reaction in a state where a new colonial power – with the same force, but different means – has changed the tribune. The appreciative talk used by those interviewed should also be seen in relation to people who, in having past experiences of dictatorship, are perhaps more inclined to be compliant when somebody, who they might perceive as a representative of the new power, begins asking questions.

"The Cold War is not over; its influence is felt even now," writes Katherine Verdery in a discussion on how else one can understand the political and scientific interest in "privatization", "marketization" and "democratization" imposed on the ex-socialist "Other" (2002: 20). In line with Verdery, I argue that cultural research has a lot to contribute in the analysis of the microprocesses of neocolonialism and neocapitalism. In the prevailing case this happens to concern the intricacies of quotidian practices around foreign investment in a postsocialist country. But, it can just as well concern places far beyond Europe, where neoliberal reforms radically transfigure both culture and living conditions for single individuals. Postsocialism, then, is part of a global phenomenon (Owczarzak 2009: 4).

Notes

1 www.swedishtrade.se, accessed October 15, 2002. All translations in this article were made by the author.

2 The characteristics of the colonial discourse are nicely drawn in Marianna Torgovnick's analysis (1990: 26–34) of Henry Stanley's book *In the Darkest of Africa*. In the same way as Stanley, the Swedish entrepreneurs encounter a foreign land with the authoritative gaze. They see a virgin, but simultaneously chaotic state in need of restoration and cultivation, something which is presumed not to be possible without Western guidance (cf. Loomba 1998: 43ff.).

3 In this experience, the foreign entrepreneurs could relate to an overarching discourse in the postsocialist context. The years after Latvian independence in 1991 is often vernacularly called "the time of confusion" (cf. Humphrey 2002).

4 www.vikawood.lv/eng/company/history/, accessed October 12, 2011.

5 Uppland is a province located slightly north of Stockholm, on the East coast of Sweden.

6 www.telia.com/~u18341401/1hist.htm, accessed March 9, 2008.

7 This article is based on three multidisciplinary research projects focusing on postsocialist cultural change in the Baltic Sea region, with a particular emphasis on Latvia: Nations and Unions: A Multidisciplinary Project on National Identity and Transnational Movements in the Baltic States (cf. Lindqvist 2003); Senmoderna avtryck: Transnationalism och kulturella förändringar i Östersjöområdet (Lindqvist & Lindqvist 2008); Global kapitalism och vardagliga motståndsformer i gränssnittet mellan Öst och Väst (cf. Lindqvist 2010, as well as the present article).

8 In line with the theorization of Banjerjee and Lindstead, I define neocolonialism as an intersection between the discourses of colonialism and globalization – an articulation that makes globalization equivalent to precisely this kind of new global colonization (2001: 694). From this point of view, power is not based on political conquest and control, but, rather, on economic and ideological dominance (see also Glick Schiller 2006).

9 Cf. Soyuz' (Post-Communist Cultural Studies Interest Group) presentation at the symposium "Walls and Bridges: Refiguring Socialist and Postsocialist Spaces in a Deterritorializing World," held at Bryant University, March 3–5, 2006.

10 The Cold War constituted a foundation, not only for neocolonialism, but also for postcolonial studies as such. The Cold War forced the West to expropriate countries and regions that were (as yet) not dominated by the Soviet empire. Likewise, the Soviet Union acted in a similar manner as a colonial power, annexing the republics and satellite states that kept the West at a comfortable distance from the centre of the empire (Verdery 2002: 18).

11 At the same time, Charles Woolfson points out the uncertainty as to whether the market reforms have been to the benefit of the working people to the same extent as it has the elites. The reforming zeal has, amongst other things, resulted in an increased unemployment, raising social inequalities, low wages, poor working conditions, insecure employment conditions, corruption and labour emigration (2008: 81).

12 Since the Eastern European revolution was a bourgeoisie revolution without a bourgeoisie – which is often claimed – there was an available place in the new social structure for foreign owners to occupy (see, e.g., Bohle 2006: 75–76).

13 In a discussion of the characteristics of socialist nations, Verdery writes: "Subjects were presumed to be neither politically active, as with citizenship, nor ethnically similar to each other: they were presumed to be grateful recipients – like small children in a family – of benefits the rulers decided upon them. The subject disposition this produced was dependency, rather than agency cultivated by citizenship or the solidarity of ethnonationalism" (1993: 45).

14 This informal spirit – whereby employees, regardless of position, are called by their first names – is also called "Scandinavian", as it is said to be commonly practiced by Nordic employers (Sippola 2006: 92).

15 www.vikawood.lv/eng/, accessed May 6, 2003.

16 www.vikawood.lv/eng/company/history/, accessed May 6, 2003.

17 The establishment of the sawmill was preceded by the purchase of wooded areas in Latvia. This serves to highlight the colonial character I find to be characteristic of this process.

18 As a result of a continuous polarization between left and right during the twentieth century it has become "common-sense" that the job market is represented by two opposing parties: work and capital, that is, of unions and employer organizations. On the political arena, this bisection has been reflected in the existence of leftist political parties versus right-wing oriented parties. The hallmark of the Swedish model in relation to these areas was the establishment of a will to compromise and peaceful coexistence, where official agreements were made and conflicts solved by way of peaceful negotiations.

19 This does not mean that Nordic unions have not assisted their Baltic counterparts. On the contrary, they have been quite intense in providing material support, education and recruitment campaigns since 1990, but they have been defensive and not very successful. It is symptomatic that Markku Sippola writes that the fundamental reason for their engagement was triggered by the danger, perceived by the Nordic union movement, of the existence of a "union free zone". The danger of [companies'] movement was the incentive (2006: 10).

20 In light of Daina Egliti's and Tana Lace's sociological depiction of the current situation on the Latvian countryside, with vast numbers of unemployment and extensive poverty, it is likely that the fact that one has a relatively safe form of employment is reason enough to be content with one's own situation (2009: 332).

21 One of the migrants says the following about the advantages of holding employment in Ireland: "In Ireland I have a job, I feel stable – I will get my wage on time; If I know my rights, then there are responsible government institutions that will help me if they are violated" (Indans et al. 2007: 24, in Eglitis & Lace 2009: 342). It is easy to see the similarity with the Vika Wood workers' judge-

ments of the advantages of the Swedish-owned company.

22 Vika Wood was sold to the Icelandic wood processing concern Norvik. The company is still an economic success story, with an annual production (2010) of 281,000 cubic metres of sawn goods (www.vikawood.lv/eng/company/history, accessed October 12, 2011).

23 www.norvik.com/en/news/100-press-release-from-vika-wood-ltd, accessed October 12, 2011.

24 Flextronics' organization resembles the world order that has followed in the wake of globalization, and that Hardt and Negri have named *Empire*, which is mainly characterized by the trait that sovereignty no longer has any territorial centre: "In contrast to imperialism, Empire establishes no territorial centre of power and does not rely on fixed boundaries or barriers. It is a decentred and deterritorializing apparatus of rule that progressively incorporates the entire global realm within its open, expanding frontiers" (2000: xii).

References

Andersen, S.K. 2006: Nordic Metal Trade Unions on the Move: Responses to Globalization and Europeanization. *European Journal of Industrial Relations* 12, 29–47.

Banerjee, S.B. & S. Linstead 2001: Globalization, Multiculturalism and Other Fictions: Colonialism for the New Millennium? *Organization* 8, 683–722.

Berdahl, D. 2005: The Spirit of Capitalism and the Boundaries of Citizenship in Post-Wall Germany. *Comparative Studies in Society and History* 47:2, 235–251.

Bergkvist, U. 2006: *Sågspån Krutrök: Och en släng av rimlåda.* Stora Enso Grycksbo: Multiart.

Bohle, D. 2006: Neoliberal Hegemony, Transnational Capital and the Terms of the EU's Eastward Expansion. *Capital & Class* 30, 57–86.

Buchowski, M. 2006: The Specter of Orientalism in Europe: From Exotic Other to Stigmatized Brother. *Anthropological Quarterly* 79:3, 463–482.

Burawoy, M. & K. Verdery (eds.) 1999: *Uncertain Transition: Ethnographies of Change in the Postsocialist World.* Lanham, MD: Rowman and Littlefield.

Castells, M. 1996: *The Information Age: Economy, Society and Culture. Vol. 1, The Rise of the Network Society.* Malden, Mass.: Blackwell.

Dalademokraten, April 13, 2004.

Domanski, B. 2004: West and East in "New Europe": The Pitfalls of Paternalism and a Claimant Attitude. *European Urban and Regional Studies* 11, 377–381.

Eglitis, D. & T. Lace 2009: Stratification and the Poverty of Progress in Post-Communist Latvian Capitalism. *Acta Sociologica* 52, 329–349.

Falu Kuriren, September 21, 2006.

Frykman, J. & O. Löfgren 1987: *Culture Builders: A Historical Anthropology of Middle-Class Life.* New Brunswick: Rutgers University Press.

Glick Schiller, N. 2006: Introduction: What Can Transnational Studies Offer the Analysis of Localized Conflict and Protest? *Focaal* 47, 3–17.

Hann, C. (ed.) 2002: *Postsocialism: Ideals, Ideologies and Practices in Eurasia.* London & New York: Routledge.

Hardt, M. & A. Negri 2000: *Empire.* London: Harvard University Press.

Harvey, D. 1989: *The Condition of Postmodernity.* Cambridge & Oxford: Blackwell.

Harvey, D. 2005: *A Brief History of Neoliberalism.* Oxford: Oxford University Press.

Harvey, D. 2007: Neoliberalism as Creative Destruction. *The Annals of the American Academy of Political and Social Science* 610:1, 22–44.

Hassler, B. 2003: *Science and Politics of Foreign Aid: Swedish Environmental Support to the Baltic States.* Dordrecht: Kluwer Academic Publishers.

Herd, G.P. & J. Löfgren 2001: 'Societal Security', the Baltic States and EU Integration. *Cooperation and Conflict* 36.

Hörschelmann, K. 2002: History after the End: Post-Socialist Difference in a (Post)modern World. *Transactions of the Institute of British Geographers* 27, 52–66.

Hörschelmann, K. & A. Stenning 2008: Ethnograhies of Postsocialist Change. *Progress in Human Geography* 32, 339–361.

Hort, S. 1994: *The Swedish Model.* Stockholm University: Department of Sociology.

Humphrey, C. 2002: *The Unmaking of Soviet Life: Everyday Economies after Socialism.* Ithaca, NY: Cornell University Press.

Kalb, D. 2002: Afterword: Globalism and Postsocialist Prospects. In: C. Hann (ed.), *Postsocialism: Ideals, Ideologies and Practices in Eurasia.* London & New York: Routledge, pp. 317–334.

Kasmir, S. 1999: The Mondragón Model as Post-Fordist Discourse: Considerations on the Production of Post-Fordism. *Current Anthropology* 19, 379.

Kideckel, D.A. 2002: The Unmaking of an East-Central European Working Class. In: C. Hann (ed.), *Postsocialism: Ideals, Ideologies and Practices in Eurasia.* London & New York: Routledge, pp. 114–132.

Kjellberg, A. 2009: The Swedish Ghent System and Trade Unions under Pressure. *Transfer: European Review of Labour and Research* 15.

Kubicek, P. 2004: *Organized Labor in Postcommunist States.* Pittsburgh: University of Pittsburgh Press.

Lindqvist, B. & M. Lindqvist 2008: *När kunden är kung: Effekter av en transnationell ekonomi.* Umeå: Boréa Förlag.

Lindqvist, M. (ed.) 2003: *Reinventing the Nation: Multidisciplinary Perspectives on the Construction of Latvian National Identity.* Botkyrka: Multicultural Centre.

Lindqvist, M. 2010: Fast and Flexible: Companies Cross Borders in the Baltic Sea Region. In: M. Hurd (ed.), *Bordering the Baltic: Scandinavian Boundary-Drawing Processes.*

Berlin: Lit Verlag, pp. 151–173.

Loomba, A. 1998: *Colonialism/Postcolonialism: The New Critical Idiom*. London & New York: Routledge.

Mandel, R. & C. Humphrey 2002: *Market & Moralities: Ethnographies of Postsocialism*. Oxford & New York: Berg.

Miller, D. 1997: *Capitalism: An Ethnographic Approach*. Oxford & New York: Berg.

Ong, A. 1987: *Spirits of Resistance and Capitalist Discipline: Factory Woman in Malaysia*. Albany: State University of New York Press.

Ong, A. 2006: Experiments with Freedom: Milieus of the Human. *American Literary History* 18, 229–244.

Ost, D. 2009: The Consequences of Postcommunism: Trade Unions in Eastern Europe's Future. *East European Politics and Societies* 23, 13–33.

Owczarzak, J. 2009: Introduction: Postcolonial Studies and Postsocialism in Eastern Europe. *Focaal* 53, 3–19.

Pajares, M. 2008: Foreign Workers and Trade Unions: The Challenges Posed. *Transfer: European Review of Labour and Research* 14, 607–624.

Picard, S. 2008: European Implications of the Laval un Partneri Dispute with Swedish Labour. *European Journal of Industrial Relations* 12.

Polanyi, K. (1944)2002: *Den stora omdaningen: Marknadsekonomins uppgång och fall*. Lund: Arkiv förlag.

Rothstein, F.A. & M. Blim (eds.) 1992: *Anthropology and the Global Factory: Studies of the New Industrialism in the Late Twentieth Century*. New York: Praeger.

Sippola, Markku 2006: *Social Dialogue in Nordic Manufacturing Companies in the Baltic States: A Work Organisation Approach*. University of Jyväskylä: Social and Public Policy Department of Social Sciences.

Sverke, M. & J. Hellgren (eds.) 2002: *Medlemmen, facket och flexibiliteten: Svensk fackföreningsrörelse i det moderna arbetslivet*. Lund: Arkiv förlag.

Torgovnick, M. 1990: *Gone Primitive: Savage Intellects, Modern Lives*. Chicago: University of Chicago Press.

Venn, C. 2009: Neoliberal Political Economy, Biopolitics and Colonialism: A Transcolonial Genealogy of Inequality. *Theory, Culture and Society* 26, 206–233.

Verdery, K. 1993: Whiter "nation" and "nationalism"? *Daedalus* 122:3, 37–46.

Verdery, K. 1996: Nationalism, Postsocialism, and Space in Eastern Europe. *Social Research* 63:1, 77–95.

Verdery, K. 2002: Whiter Postsocialism? In: C. Hann (ed.), *Postsocialism: Ideals, Ideologies and Practices in Eurasia*. London & New York: Routledge, pp. 15–22.

Woolfson, C. 2008: Social Dialogue and Lifelong Learning in New EU Member States: "Reform Fit" in Latvia. *Journal of European Social Policy* 18:1, 79–87.

Woolfson, C. & J. Sommers 2006: Labour Mobility in Construction: European Implications of the Laval un Partneri Dispute with Swedish Labour. *European Journal of Industrial Relations* 12, 49–68.

Mats Lindqvist is Professor of Ethnology at Södertörn University in Stockholm, Sweden. He has produced books and articles about the construction of national identity, the culture of capitalism and workers culture in late-modern industries. See *Re-inventing the Nation: Multidisciplinary Perspectives on the Construction of Latvian National Identity* (ed.), 2003; *The Story of Progress* (ed. together with Gösta Arvastson), 1996; and "Quick and Flexible: Companies Cross Borders in the Baltic Sea Region", in: Madeleine Hurd (ed.), *Bordering the Baltic*, 2010.
(mats.lindqvist@sh.se)

BENEATH THE SURFACE OF THE HERITAGE ENTERPRISE

Governmentality and Cultural Representation of Rural Architecture in Portugal

Luís Silva

This article focuses on the construction of heritage in rural Portugal. Drawing on anthropological fieldwork in the village of Castelo Rodrigo, it analyses the extensive protection and exhibition of domestic architecture in the framework of a State-led local development programme. By bringing in the messiness of daily practices, the article goes beyond neat theoretical formulations in the study of heritage such as Foucault's theory of "governmentality" and Kirshenblatt-Gimblett's notion of "second life as heritage". It argues that the "conduct of conduct" is actually nowhere near as effective as its theoretical formulation might have us believe, and the second life as heritage suffocates the first life of houses as social habitats for the village population.

Keywords: architectural heritage, "governmentality", "second life as heritage", second homes, Portugal

This text provides an analysis of the contemporary construction of cultural heritage in rural areas. The main aim is to find out what happens when houses that are being lived in are converted into heritage. Who constructs built heritage, how is it constructed and why? What impact does the construction of heritage have on the social context? And how is the protection of housing as heritage reconciled with people's need to live in the buildings? Pursuing these questions in rural Portugal, the article delves beneath the surface of the heritage enterprise into the untidy details of how things actually work out on the ground. Hence, it will contribute to clarifying the problematic transformation of private and family properties into public heritage, and also to giving an account of the power relations that characterise these processes (Graham, Ashworth & Tunbridge 2000, Gravari-Barbas 2005, Herzfeld 1991; Macleod 2010).

My discussion is grounded on anthropological fieldwork conducted in the first half of 2009 in the rural village of Castelo Rodrigo.[1] Ideas of historical conservation emerged here as early as 1922; at that time, the ruins of the castle and of fortress walls as well as the *Manueline*[2] pillory were accorded official protection status as a "national monument". Subsequently, in 1961, the church of Rocamador was accorded official protection status as a "building of public interest".[3] More recently, in 1995, historical conservation was extended to the entire urban environment within and around the fortress walls. Changes were then made to privately-owned architecture on the facades and roofs, in patterns that prefigure a re-traditionalisation. Moreover, the urban fabric became subject to the exigencies of historical conservation.

This article shows that both the intervention on private buildings and the exigencies of historical conservation are intrinsically problematic since historic conservationists and most residents have rather different views on housing and thus different portfolios of intervention in the buildings.[4] It is a clear example of how individuals and social groups struggle to manage and control space, in order to pursue their particular interests (Lefebvre [1974]1991, [1972]1976). Nowadays, almost all residents feel proud to live in a classified village, which is "clean, pretty and restored." They reproduce the rhetoric of historical conservation when it suits them to do so. For example, they argue that the State or the municipal government should restore all buildings located in the old town centre because of their historical value, that is, "because they are very old." Yet they resist this official appropriation of their living spaces, particularly their own homes, and adamantly criticise the rhetoric of historical conservation when it runs counter to their interests.

The Setting and the Context

The village of Castelo Rodrigo is part of the municipality of Figueira de Castelo Rodrigo, some 70 kilometres from the city of Guarda in eastern Portugal. The administrative centre of the *freguesia* (parish) that bears its name is a walled village situated at the top of a hill, at about 820 metres above sea level.

Castelo Rodrigo is in various ways an example of the socioeconomic transformation that rural areas of Portugal have been undergoing during the last sixty years. For a start, there has been a decline in the number of people living off primary sector economic activities, particularly agriculture, as well as a consequent exodus to major cities in Portugal, and farther afield to other countries such as Mozambique, France and Germany. Although exact figures are unavailable for Castelo Rodrigo, the inhabitants remember that the village where "there had not been enough houses for everyone and many people had lived in barns" in the mid-twentieth century, had become "very depopulated and had turned into a pile of ruins" by the early 1970s. In the 1970s, the village experienced a temporary population growth due (principally) to the arrival of *retornado* families who returned to Portugal after the independence of the former Portuguese colonies in Africa, particularly Mozambique. During the following years exodus was once again the order of the day for the village.

In the 1990s, the decline in economic activity in Castelo Rodrigo began to be combated. Some independent individuals, as well as the local government and the municipal government, started to earn money by receiving a growing number of tourists in search of cultural tourism experiences.[5] The first tourism business was set up by Lurdes Saraiva, a former primary-school teacher in her sixties, shortly after she moved into her mother's house. She started the business in partnership with a younger sister, also a school teacher. In 1993, they began to offer accommodation services in a "traditional" house in the village; the house is the result of the extension and adaptation of an old stone house and a barn. The initiative was preceded and followed by other initiatives, both public and private, aiming to take advantage of the economic value of heritage (Bendix 2009; Graham, Ashworth & Tunbridge 2000: 17, 20–22; Kirshenblatt-Gimblett 1998). Since 2002, the tourism industry has begun to modestly flourish in the village, both in terms of demand and supply.[6]

At present, tourism is the principal economic activity for six (9 percent) permanent residents – most of them recent internal migrants – and also up to ten individuals who do not live in the village, including three tourist entrepreneurs. Most of the employed population work in services, public administration and commerce in Figueira de Castelo Rodrigo, some two kilometres from the village; the others work in the ceramics factory near Castelo Rodrigo, construction, transport, agriculture, and also at the archaeological park of Foz Côa, classified as a World Heritage Site by Unesco in 1998.

In general, the residents have a positive view of tourism and tourists, particularly because they provide extra income to some people – albeit seasonally and usually falling short of expectations and wishes. However, they complain about sacrificing their own interests, particularly in relation to their homes, in favour of the interests of the tourism sector.

Political Power and Rural Architecture

The municipal government of Figueira de Castelo Rodrigo has played a leading role in developing cultural tourism in the village. This role commenced in the early 1990s, when the municipal government promoted the preservation of the fortress walls and of the castle – which includes the ruins of the palace of Cristóvão de Moura (1538–1613)[7] – in partnership with the national body in charge of these monuments. The project of the municipal political leaders would have a decisive impetus in 1995 with the integration of Castelo Rodrigo into a national programme, entitled *Programa de Recuperação de Aldeias Históricas de Portugal* (Recovery Programme for the Historic Villages of Portugal).

This programme forms part of rural development policies that have been promoting the growth of tourism in the rural areas of Portugal and other developed countries since the early 1990s (Abram & Waldren 1998; Jenkins, Hall & Troughton 1998; OECD 1994; Silva 2009a). Indeed, it sought to increase cultural tourism in twelve rural villages adversely affected by the de-ruralisation process. The aim was to preserve historic built heritage and, above all, use it as a lever of social and economic development though its tourist commoditisation. This comprises not only elements of military and religious architecture, such as castles and churches, but also elements of folk architecture, such as houses and barns (Silva 2009b).

Designed by the national government and the Commission for the Development and Coordination of the Central Region, the Historic Villages of Portugal programme was implemented – with European Union Funding – between 1995 and 2006, in cooperation with the historic conservation agencies (the former Portuguese Institute of Architectural Heritage and the former General Board of National Buildings and Monuments[8]), the National Institute for the Advantageous Use of Workers' Free Time, municipalities, and private actors.

The village of Castelo Rodrigo entered the programme because it met the criteria of "the existence of classified architectural heritage" and "historic and cultural interest." Presented by the municipal government to the coordinating body, the Commission for the Development and Coordination of the Central Region, the application was based on the village plan designed by a team of architects from the city of Oporto, whose leader designed the "memorial of the ruins" in the castle and palace. The village plan identified what work was to be done in the village and in the built environment, private buildings included. The ultimate goal was to display them for tourism, in a process that John Urry would describe as "designing for the gaze" (Urry 1999: 220). In his view, "architects and architectural practices are of major importance in shaping the contemporary tourist gaze" (ibid.: 220).[9] In the village of Castelo Rodrigo this can be clearly observed.

The built environment was put on display for tourists by architects, both the architects that designed the village plan and those working for historic conservation bodies. Almost all building projects were subject to tensions and power relations, particularly the church of Rocamador and the public lighting.[10] But the most contentious ones were those related to houses, which are the object of study in this text. To further understand the situation, it is important to look back in time and to move away from Castelo Rodrigo.

Interest in rural folk architecture emerged in the late nineteenth century, in a context marked by the impact of industrialisation on architecture, as well as by practices of national identity building (Lowenthal 1985, 1998; Samuel 1994). As shown by several authors (Leal 2000; Sobral 2004), in Portugal, as in other European countries, forms of rural architecture were converted into emblems of national identity, not only among the intellectuals who were debating the nation from the late nineteenth century until the 1970s, but also within the political regime of the *Estado Novo* (New State) dictatorship (1927–1974). For example, housing was one of the main criteria for measuring the *portugalidade* (Portugueseness) of the villages that competed in the *Aldeia mais por-*

tuguesa de Portugal (Most Portuguese Village) competition launched by the dictatorial regime in 1938.

There has been renewed interest in forms of rural architecture during the last thirty years, but in a different context. The aim is to promote cultural tourism, understood as a lever of socioeconomic development. In Portugal, as in other European countries, governments at all administrative levels have invested money to capitalise on forms of rural architecture, no longer understood as symbols of the nation, but rather of the place, of local heritage and culture (cf. Lindknud 1998; Rautenberg 2003). Here one witnesses a shift from heritage produced to trigger national identity to heritage produced for tourist consumption and economic profit (Rowan & Baram 2004). In Portugal, this can be visibly observed in the accommodation sector officially known as *Turismo no Espaço Rural* (Tourism in the Rural Space); this is a type of small-scale and familial tourist accommodation that includes agro-tourism (Silva 2009a, 2010). But it can also be seen in many political programmes that rehabilitate buildings and even entire villages for tourism in rural villages of the interior. This is the case, for example, of the *Villages of Saudade* in Minho, the *Villages of Xystus* in the central region, the *Water Villages* in Alentejo, and the *Historic Villages of Portugal* in the central region, which includes Castelo Rodrigo.

Barbara Kirshenblatt-Gimblett's theorisation of heritage provides a useful tool to better understand the process. In her point of view, heritage practices endow objects, buildings, sites, technologies and ways of life with a "second life as heritage", a life "as exhibits of themselves". Having exhausted the initial function – the first life – they acquire new functions and values, or they are reborn as displays of what they once were. Moreover, the "rebirth" is intimately related to tourism, for tourism makes economically viable "as representations of themselves" buildings and practices that "can no longer sustain themselves as they formerly did" (Kirshenblatt-Gimblett 1998: 149–151).

In this theoretical formulation, the two lives of buildings, objects and practices converted into heritage follow each other. This is the case, for example, of material culture displayed in museums, as well as of derelict buildings converted into tourist accommodations. However, there are cases in which the second life of buildings and practices is concurrent with the first life. This applies, for example, to private architecture in Castelo Rodrigo – the houses serve simultaneously as homes for the village population and as representations of themselves, having both a first life as social habitats and a second life as heritage. It is the co-occurrence of first and second life in the same objects that I want to explore here.

The Two Lives of Housing

From the nineteenth until the mid-twentieth century in Castelo Rodrigo, domestic architecture tended to be built from local materials such as granite stone and mortar, often with rocky outcrops at the base; some houses were built into the fortress walls. Terraces were constructed over these, which obstructed the surrounding thoroughfare. As in other borderland rural villages in the central and northern regions of Portugal, the houses used to have two floors – the ground floor and the first floor. Typically, the ground floor was used for keeping animals or for the installation of the winepress and cellar, which not all residents possessed, particularly not the poorest among them. In some cases, there was also a bunk where single male children slept, while females slept in the bedroom. In addition, there was an "ashtray" where the ashes of the fireplace on the first floor were laid and thereafter used as fertiliser. The first floor also had a kitchen and one or two bedrooms. The doors and windows were made of wood and the roofs were supported by wooden beams, without slabs of reinforced concrete. To increase insulation, the more affluent owners tended to cover the stonework of the facades with mortar and whitewash, unlike the poor, who kept them uncovered.

Things started to change in the first decades of the twentieth century with the use of industrial or mass-produced materials, such as brick, concrete and aluminium, and the widespread use of whitewash and ink paints. The use of industrial materials on buildings became commonplace in the 1970s and 1980s. This was the result of action by various groups of individuals then linked to the village: the *retornado* families; those who settled to work at the ceramics factory and other craftspeople; those who had immigrated, principally to France, and had built a home in the village with the money earned there; and those who lived continuously in Castelo Rodrigo.

They all invested in improving the living conditions of the old stone houses where they were born and lived – houses that were usually small, dark and with few rooms, separated by small partitions made of straw and clay. They had no electricity, running water or bathrooms;[11] in addition, the interior walls were blackened by smoke from the fireplace which the crudely-built chimney did not properly expel. This type of construction was not confined to the most modest homes; it was equally present in the homes of "rich people", the main landowners, and the church. Therefore, many owners have added one floor of brick and reinforced concrete to the old stone houses; they have also replaced the old wooden doors and windows of the facade with new ones made from aluminium and iron; and they have transformed the ground floors into garages, bedrooms or storage rooms. Some of the poorer residents have built their houses by vertically expanding old barns, while some of the more affluent have expanded them horizontally by combining them with adjoining buildings.

In most cases, the houses were constructed in stages, according to the economic power of the owners: first the kitchen, then the bedrooms and the bathroom. The inhabitants of that period remember that "it was a time when everyone was building the houses in whatever way they could." Modern materials represented novelty and were cheaper than traditional ones; the inhabitants of that period recall that "it was cheaper to make a brick wall than to make a stone wall," as it is today. To sum up, the owners have been renovating and building their houses according to various factors, such as physical and social requirements, conceptions of home and domestic space, aesthetic preferences and budget constraints. Nevertheless, not all homeowners in Castelo Rodrigo have invested in the physical maintenance and improvement of their houses; many left them to fall into ruin since they left the village and do not intend to return.

The municipal government of Figueira de Castelo Rodrigo began trying to control the built environment of the village of Castelo Rodrigo in the 1940s. At that time, it banned the whitewashing of facades and all works not authorised by the municipal technical services and by the national historic conservation body. The main aim was to prevent the eruption of "modernity" into the village, in defence of the prestigious brand of the past. But neither the municipal government nor the historic conservationists could make residents comply with the rules, largely because of lack of control and means. The residents of the time remember that "nobody attached importance to the works carried out in the village, neither the municipal government, nor the [former] Portuguese Institute of Architectural Heritage." The only procedure that the municipal government saw complied with by most residents was the disguising of "modernity", through the placement of small granite stones on the facades of buildings. This includes not only homes but also storerooms and garages that residents were building inside and outside the fortress walls.

The first application to integrate Castelo Rodrigo in the Historic Villages of Portugal programme was rejected by those in charge not only because of the advanced state of ruin of most buildings, but also because of the "modern" appearance of many others. The application was approved only when the architects who designed the village plan requested an appeal and claimed that it was an excellent opportunity to correct the situation of "ruin and contamination". Since this decision of approval, both the historic conservation organisations and the municipal government have had more means and motivation at their disposal to control the built environment. This has drastically changed the evolutionary picture of domestic architecture in the village, thereby creating friction between house owners and historic conservation bodies, because the houses started to embody two different lives – a first life as social habitats for the village population and a second life as heritage.

Following a common trend in the study of heritage (Bendix & Hafstein 2009; De Cesari 2010; Hodges 2009; Smith 2004, 2006), the process could be described as a governmental practice, along the lines set out by Michel Foucault (1991, [1994]2002). For the author, the modern government of populations – "governmentality" – is exerted through "technologies" of power, that is, practices inspired and justified by one or more scientific rationales, according to contingent "strategies". In his point of view, the exercise of power is a "conduct of conduct", that is, an action that defines the possibilities for action of others (Foucault [1994]2002: 341).

Governmentality theory provides a useful framework to understand the case of Castelo Rodrigo, at least part of it. In this sense, the strategy of the national government and of the municipal government was to rationalise the built environment in order to create a tourist destination. Architectural knowledge functions as a technology of government that help to determine the conduct of individuals with respect to architecture and the aesthetic characteristics of buildings in the village. It is this organisation of space that I wish to explore now. In the process, some limitations of governmentality theory in the study of heritage will be unveiled. In brief, governmentality fails to make space for resistance and contestation to expert knowledge, and for interference in the conduct and subversion as well (see also Smith 2004).

The village plan sought to restore the buildings and return them to an earlier, premodern state; it is a process that Matt Hodges would describe as "symbolic antiquation", "through which artefacts are reconstructed as *simulacra* of an imagined former state" (Hodges 2009: 77; italics in the original). To this end, it proposed to restore the buildings and to correct the "architectural dissonances", that is, to eliminate the new and spurious elements, such as brick and aluminium, which contaminated the prestigious and legitimate materials of the past, such as stone and wood.

Michel Rautenberg's findings in the study of rural heritage in France explain the situation. Experts see vernacular architecture and industrial architecture as two different and incompatible architectures; they believe there is a *rupture* between these two architectures, in the same way they perceive a *rupture* between a traditional world and the contemporary world. By contrast, house owners see a *historical continuity* between both architectures, and they regard them as being compatible (Rautenberg 2003: 93).

This is what happened, and continues to happen, in the village of Castelo Rodrigo. Theoretically, the plan of physical intervention in buildings envisaged the following operations: restoration of facades; restoration and standardisation of roofs; removal of "modern" impurities from the facades and roofs (television antennas, balconies, gutter pipes, clothes lines and shutters); placement of wooden doors and windows in the facades; discovery of the stonework in facades with good masonry finishes; and covering of the facades with plaster and whitewash or paint in situations in which "this proves to be the original state of the building." In practice, however, things developed in a different way, for various reasons.

For a start, the work was carried out in stages and funds came to an end before the renovation of all buildings had been completed. The work began to be carried out on buildings situated on the two main streets of the village, independently of their uses and functions. Over time, 105 private buildings underwent work on their facades and roofs, both inhabited and uninhabited, of a total of around 130. Included here are around 65 houses. Less than half of the houses are permanently lived in, one third of the remainder are used only as holiday or second homes, and the rest remain abandoned. Most of them belong to local people, some resident in the village and others in other parts of the country and abroad. The others belong to urban dwellers and outsiders from nearby villages.

The village population comprises 62 permanent residents and about 40 temporary residents, a third of them over 65 years. While 69 percent of permanent residents claim to be from the village, the other 31 percent are internal migrants – over two-thirds of them settled in the 1970s, either due to marriage or for the purposes of local employment; the others settled in the 2000s to work in the tourism sector.

The temporary residents comprise villagers who live and work elsewhere in the country and abroad, particularly in France, as well as half a dozen of recent second home owners; most of these have no prior connection with the village.

Another problem which confronted architects in the implementation of the village plan was the existence of many buildings constructed entirely or partly of bricks and concrete. In these cases, if there was no demolition, the architects decided to cover the facades with plaster and orange-coloured paint, solely because the region is rich in clay. This was also the reason why the stonework of the facades was enhanced through the use of a mortar with an orange tone in the joints. Many residents criticise the use of this mortar because rainwater washes it away and, they say, it makes their homes more porous and wet because the sand is too small and allows infiltrations.

Moreover, there has been resistance from the village population. The first wave of resistance came from the owners of buildings located outside the fortress walls. The architects envisaged their total or partial demolition, as they were "modern" buildings constructed within the protection zone of the national monument; the protection zone extends to fifty metres, counted from the external limits of the artefact. But the owners prevented this action in order to keep their homes and garages. This was the case, for example, of a farming couple in their sixties, whose house had been built in the 1980s with brick and concrete. In a conversation near her home, the owner recalls experiencing a period of great anguish and despair:

> Since my childhood I had dreamed of having a house. My husband and I had worked a lifetime to realise this dream. And then the architects wanted to demolish it. I am a very anxious woman and one day, after some sleepless nights, I took my husband's gun and asked him to teach me to shoot it... if they destroy my house, I'll kill them; fortunately, this never happened.

Another example is the report of a garage owner in his late seventies, collected in one of our regular conservations near the fortress walls:

> One day the mayor of the municipal council came to me, accompanied by the architect, and said it was necessary to demolish the garage. And I told him: "you can demolish the garage, but only if you build me another one within the village." When he told me that this was not possible, I replied: "so I keep the garage."

The only work that these owners have consented to do was to remove the small granite stones that they had placed on the facades of buildings to disguise their "modernity". The residents, despite acknowledging that "the small stones do not look good in a historic village," have some difficulty in perceiving how it is possible that the authorities now want to undo work that they had made compulsory in previous years. This is the case, for example, of a resident in his early seventies who owns a "modern" house in the old town centre:

> One day the workers of the company which restored some buildings here for the Historic Villages of Portugal [programme] came to change the roof of my house (...), and put up scaffolding all around it. I approached them and said: "What are you doing?" They said: "What are we doing!? We are removing the small granite stones from the facades." And then I told them: "What the hell!? I walked so much, with my wife and a son, to find these stones, and bring them here on a donkey, to paste on the facades because the municipal government forced me, and now you rip them out... I do not understand any of this." I know that it looks better that way, but the public authorities cannot play with people.

Resistance was also the attitude of the owners of buildings located within the fortress walls, particularly at an earlier stage. Their resistance was not motivated by economic reasons since the municipal government was offering the project and covered the percentage of costs that the programme claimed to be the responsibility of private actors, ranging between 10 and 25 percent. The house owners resisted for fear of harming their own particular interests. This was because the municipal government would only fund the work if the conditions set by the architects were fulfilled; otherwise the grant was not awarded or was removed.

Meanwhile, the works were being carried out according to negotiations and power relations among concerned parties, principally architects and homeowners. As Henri Lefebvre notes, "the architect cannot simply draw, and cannot fail to consult orally (by means of the word) other actors implicated in the production of space, above all the user" (Lefebvre [1972]1976: 16). In Castelo Rodrigo, "in order to avoid conflicts," the architects and other professionals negotiated the details of the works in each particular case with the homeowners. In some cases, they had to forego their rules – and what they saw as the right conduct – in order to achieve the goal of restoring the built environment. This is what happened with the aesthetic image of the buildings. Influenced by the priest Canário Martins (1911–2005), the residents demanded the uncovering of the stonework of the facades in all buildings, including cases in which according to the architects the buildings should have been covered with plaster and whitewash or paint, as in the past. The residents' attitude is associated with a change in the meaning of visible stonework – in the past it was associated with poverty; now, instead, it stood for affluence and good taste.

There were also house owners who were able to impose conditions that ran counter to the architects' plan. For example, a man in his fifties, then a member of the local government, managed to prevent the demolition of a "modern" balcony in his house on the main street. Likewise, a man of the same age only authorised the works on his home – also on the main street – when the architects responded to his desire to raise it to the level of an adjacent small tower – which currently functions as its private garden – and to keep a skylight in the roof. Similarly, the brother of the then mayor of the local government was able to build an additional floor in his home and to keep small granite stones in the facades.

On the contrary, most residents have had to abide by the stipulations in the architects' plan. Some have seen their intentions to make an additional floor in their homes or to raise the ceiling of rooms – often to accommodate their children's families when they come to visit – rejected; others have seen "modern" additions to buildings being demolished, such as balconies; and others, finally, have not been allowed to open windows on the facades and to put skylights in roofs, even in cases where the entrance of light is very reduced.

Over time, however, some procedures adopted by experts in the display of architecture for tourism have been overturned by the residents, as they have proved to be harmful to their interests. For example, some residents reinstalled gutter pipes and clothes lines in the facades of their houses because they are useful for housing, the first life of domestic spaces as social habitats (see ill. 1). Others reinstalled television antennas or satellite dishes on rooftops because the cable television in the village works badly. Among those who can afford it, some have also replaced the wooden doors and windows on the facades with others made of aluminium – albeit of a type that looks like wood. It turns out that the wood placed at the expense of the programme is of poor quality and warps in a short time, not providing proper insulation. The residents tend to say that they were deceived by the contractor's work, but they blame the municipal government for not carrying out proper monitoring and supervision of the works; and they justify their actions by saying that they want to better insulate their homes.

The architects and historic conservation bodies have some difficulty in justifying to the residents the need to use "traditional" materials in private buildings, while at the same time using "modern" ones in public spaces. For example, they applied iron and steel in the ruins of the castle and of the palace of Cristóvão de Moura, and also in the tourist office. Moreover, they placed an aluminium door on the mortuary house built in 2001 near the church of Rocamador. They also placed aluminium windows at the headquarters of the Association for the Development of Tourism for the Historic Villages of

Ill. 1: Visible stonework and gutter pipes in the facades of houses in Castelo Rodrigo. (Photo: Luís Silva, 2009)

Portugal built in 2009 at the location of the former primary-school building outside the fortress walls. The architects acknowledge the possibility of using "modern" materials in private architecture, but only in specific cases and when the work is controlled by experts.

The bodies responsible for historic conservation in Castelo Rodrigo, namely the municipal council and the Institute for the Management of Architectural and Archaeological Heritage, have no supervisors, and they only act when someone is reported or when their officials notice something wrong. Cases of fines levied on offenders or embargoes on works have been rare. As the architect of the municipal council points out in an interview at his office in the city hall,

> We know there are misappropriations of space in Castelo Rodrigo, but we do not want to enter into open conflict with the residents. We want to keep the spaces lived in, and we know that residents have their needs. In the village, the housing conditions are difficult because of bad weather and improper insulation.

Aside from prohibiting new constructions within and around the fortress walls, the historic conservation rules severely restrict changes to the size and aesthetics of buildings. They also prohibit the installation of skylights in the roofs, and advocate the use of wooden doors and windows on the facades. Moreover, they require that all construction projects are signed off by an architect, and are subject to the judgment of the Institute for the Management of

Architectural and Archaeological Heritage. This is because the village and buildings are considered heritage that should be protected like a historic monument. And of course there is also tourism.

Tourism is also part of the rhetorical tactics used by architects in promoting respect for the historic conservation rules among the residents. They try to dissuade the residents from "damaging the village's tourist image" by carrying out inappropriate works on the buildings; they argue that by doing so residents adversely affect their own interests, because Castelo Rodrigo will no longer attract tourists. The tourist image of the village, which the tourist experience usually reiterates, as many tourists said to me during face-to-face interviews and informal conversations, is that of a "medieval village", "rustic" and "typical", as if it were suspended in a kind of a mythical past, "out of real time and place" (MacCannell [1976]1999: 41). Hence, the architects strive to promote a voluntary interruption of time and accordingly freeze private architecture in time.

The tourist entrepreneurs and recent second home owners approve the architectural protectionism. They say that "it is fine that people are not allowed to do what they want on houses because it is important to preserve the tradition and old lines of buildings." Therefore, they adamantly criticise the villagers who do not respect the rules. This is the case, for instance, of a second home owner, a lawyer in his early seventies, who usually lives in the city of Oporto:

> Many people in Castelo Rodrigo still have a Romanic conception of property law and think they can do whatever they want with the buildings, such as using aluminium on outward-facing doors and windows and keeping and putting up garages as well. We are not in Roman times anymore, but the truth is that people are spoiling our heritage.

In Kirshenblatt-Gimblett's (1998) terms, largely this is because the second life of houses as exhibits of themselves serves the private interests of both tourist entrepreneurs and second home owners; indeed, as noted above, the second life was the leitmotiv of their influx into the village arena. For the former, it is an opportunity to earn money from tourism, or to take economic advantage of "the value of exhibition" (ibid.: 151). For the latter, by contrast, it is an opportunity to realise the "dream of a second home" (Bendix & Löfgren 2008: 12) in the countryside in order to enjoy periods of leisure, and one simultaneously endowed with a second life as heritage in a prestigious heritage ensemble, such as a Historic Village of Portugal. This applies to children of residents who live and work in cities and to other affluent city dwellers as well. Moreover, they all normally live in bigger and better insulated houses – houses made of two or three adjoining buildings and, in many cases, equipped with "modern" heating equipment and double-glazed windows in the facades; with these windows, they subvert the same cultural representation of housing as heritage that they advocate.

By contrast, most permanent residents resist the official appropriation of their living spaces, and strive to continue transforming the houses according to the needs and possibilities of the present. In other words, they strive to defend their first life as social habitats for the village population. They even say that "we are no longer masters of our own homes, and we cannot change them except as they [the historic conservationists] want." They recognise the importance of the tourist image and the need for architectural rules, but they object to how strict those rules are and thus contest the conduct of conduct.

To further understand the situation, we must take into account that most houses are still quite small; many houses also have rocky outcrops in the interior that make the situation worse. In addition, their internal design does not conform to the physical and social requirements of a modern family, such as the need for plenty of light and individual bedrooms. Few residents indeed can afford to expand them either upwards or sideways because the historic conservation rules are restrictive of changes in the size of buildings and, principally, the house prices are very high. In the course of fieldwork I met three young couples who went to live in other places, principally Figueira de Castelo Rodrigo, precisely for these reasons.

Here one witnesses more clearly how the second life as exhibits of themselves suffocates the first life of houses as social habitats for the village population. The proliferation of tourism businesses and, principally, the increased level of second home ownership are actually hindering the social reproduction of the village population because they have raised the price of housing to the extent that local people can no longer afford to buy houses and the younger ones move away to other areas. The influx of wealthier individuals into Castelo Rodrigo is evident in the words of one resident in his fifties: "this village never had so many rich people as nowadays: a couple of judges, a lawyer, and five doctors."

These are the main reasons why many permanent residents contend that they had to sacrifice their housing conditions for the benefit of the official version of the past and a tourist image. The testimony of one resident in her early seventies illustrates the point:

> I wanted to raise the ceiling of a bedroom by fifty centimetres, because we cannot stand up right. One day the architects and an engineer working for the Historic Villages of Portugal programme at the expense of the municipal government came to me, and I showed them the bedroom. Then, they told me: "you cannot do it because it is forbidden to change the appearance of the houses in order to preserve the history of the village and also because of tourism." I was furious, and I replied: "people do not live *from* appearances; the village's history is the history of the past, present and future residents; what you are doing is turning Castelo Rodrigo into a ghost village, just with tourist accommodations and second homes, where some individuals come to stay a few days twice a year."

The words of this lady also give good reason to refer back to Barbara Kirshenblatt-Gimblett's (1998) formulation that in their second life as heritage, the buildings, objects and practices become representations of themselves. She says that "people do not live from appearances," and then goes on to accuse the architects of "turning Castelo Rodrigo into a ghost village." Here the notion of second life seems particularly fruitful, for of course second life may also refer to the afterlife. Ghosts, and ghost villages, may be thought of as a form of afterlife – "appearances". Perhaps better yet, ghosts are often conceived of in popular tradition to be caught between this life and the afterlife, between their first and second life, much as is the case with the houses in Castelo Rodrigo.

Conclusion

The aim of this article was to understand what happens when domestic architecture is converted into cultural heritage by public authorities, in order to create tourist destinations. In other words, it set out to provide an ethnographic case study of the untidy details of how things actually work out on the ground when the heritage enterprise touches a space that is being lived in, and how this affects the social context. Theoretically, it speaks directly to Michel Foucault's (1991) theory of "governmentality" and to Barbara Kirshenblatt-Gimblett's (1998) notion of "second life as heritage". The study focuses on the rural village of Castelo Rodrigo in eastern Portugal.

From the perspective of governmentality theory, here one could see heritage as an act of government that mobilises expert technologies to define architecture as an object of touristic consumption and therefore to determine the conduct of conduct. The village plan could be seen as a pedagogical and disciplinary tool that architects designed to help to create appropriate buildings for tourism. The rules for architecture and the aesthetic characteristics of buildings could also be seen as having a similar disciplinary function in the village.

However, from the outcomes of the research, it is evident that, although useful for the study of heritage, governmentality theory does not provide an exact account of how things actually work out on the ground. Here is rich ethnographic evidence that the conduct of conduct is actually nowhere near as effective as its theoretical formulation might have us believe. There is friction in the channels, interference in the conduct, contestation, dissent, resistance and subversion, as well as compromise. The agendas of the central government do not translate neatly into the technologies of experts and local authorities, though translation does take place, nor do these effectively shape the everyday practices of residents, though they do have a considerable effect.

In Castelo Rodrigo, architecture has become a major arena for social conflict in which different types of power relations are played out: the public authorities which initiated the heritage-making process; the experts who intend to shape the conduct of individuals; the building companies; the legal owners and users of houses; and the tourist entrepreneurs. Depending on circumstances, they all make use of or withdraw their power relations in order to promote their particular and often divergent interests. Ultimately, it is this struggle that governmentality theory fails to make room for in the study of heritage, as Laurajane Smith (2004) aptly reports with respect to archaeological expertise and knowledge in postcolonial settler societies such as Australia and the United States of America.

The data from Castelo Rodrigo also adds nuance to Kirshenblatt-Gimblett's (1998) theorisation of heritage as the second life of objects, buildings and practices as representations of themselves. Here one witnesses that the second life as heritage is not solely attributed to "obsolete", "outmoded", "dead" and "defunct" objects, buildings and practices as the theoretical formulation indicates, for the houses serve simultaneously as homes for the village population and as representations of themselves, having both a first life as social habitats and a second life as heritage. As it has also become clear in the article, the co-occurrence of first and second life in the same buildings is cause of friction between individuals and social groups with different interests. In brief, the historic conservation advocates strive to defend the second life of houses as exhibits of themselves, while most residents strive to defend the first life of their homes as dynamic social habitats which they want to continue to transform according to the needs and possibilities of the present.

Moreover, in Castelo Rodrigo the second life actually suffocates the first life. First, it freezes buildings in time, whereas previously they had been constantly changing. Consequently, most residents are unable to continue to make improvements to their small houses because of restrictive disciplinary measures. Second, and principally, it hinders the social reproduction of the village population because it has raised the price of houses – and other buildings – to the extent that local people can no longer afford to buy houses and the younger ones move away to other areas. In addition to planning policies that prohibit new construction within and around the fortress walls, this is the result of the influx of wealthier individuals into the village arena, looking for tourism businesses and, principally, for second homes, as is often the case in popular rural areas (cf. Sharpley & Sharpley 1997: 142).

The connexion between the second life as heritage and tourism is hardly surprising, for of course they are interdependent (Kirshenblatt-Gimblett 1998: 151). It is also no big surprise that tourism has modest effects on the local economy, and falling short of expectations and wishes. Indeed, in Portugal the effective contribution of tourism in rural regeneration tends to be reduced (Cavaco 1995; Silva 2009a, 2010), as it is often the case in Western Europe, although some authors might have us believe the opposite (e.g., Greffe 1994; Timothy & Boyd 2003: 45–46, 171, 187). What is remarkable is the connexion between the second life as heritage and second homes, although some authors regard them as a form of tourism (Jaakson 1986; Sharpley & Sharpley 1997; Strapp 1988). In Castelo Rodrigo, the main appeal of the second home is its second life as heritage. In addition, the second life proved to be better suited for a second home than for a first home, for different reasons.

On the one hand, the physical and social requirements of a modern family such as the need for plenty of light and ample space are somehow not as important in second homes as in first homes, for of course people spend more time in a first home than in a second home, particularly those attributable to leisure pursuits – although a second home may become a first home over the course of time (Bendix & Löfgren 2008: 14); as a lady quoted above says, in Castelo Rodrigo most second home owners "come to stay for a few days twice a year." On the other hand, the second home owners overtly defend the cultural representation of houses as exhibits of themselves that attracts them. Normally, the appeal of vernacular architecture is also mirrored in the interior of houses, which the owners furnish with what they describe as "antique" and "rustic" objects, much like the facades.

The lesson we learn from Castelo Rodrigo may also help in understanding other places and heritage practices in general. The dissonant and contested nature of heritage (see Tunbridge & Ashworth 1996; Graham, Ashworth & Tunbridge 2000; Herzfeld 1991; Smith 2006) is particularly strong when it focuses on cultural resources that are being lived in and are deemed to be inalienable possessions by a segment of the owners and practitioners, and are seen as resources for tourism or collective memory by others. The same objects, buildings and practices then become a major arena for social tension and conflict between individuals and groups with different interests and points of view regarding their purposes.

With respect to housing, heritage advocates strive to create a fixed cultural representation of domestic architecture and thus to control architecture and the aesthetic characteristics of buildings. By contrast, most homeowners resist the official appropriation of their social habitats, for various reasons. First, the new set of rules and interdictions surrounding heritage changes their lifetime practices of building and transforming houses according to contingent circumstances. Second, they see it as an illegitimate interference in private domains, which runs counter to their particular interests, for the houses no longer provide appropriate living conditions as they once did. Third, they do not benefit significantly from heritage-making, and do not feel compensated by the corresponding constraints. Heritage practices normally do not improve the living conditions and livelihoods of ordinary people, since the work on the buildings tends to focus on facades and roofs, and the economic benefits of tourism accrue mainly to the more affluent and influential residents. Fourth, they may feel resentful of the fact that their place has been taken over by wealthy outsiders looking for tourism businesses and second homes, and they have to move away because of high house prices and restrictive disciplinary measures.

Thus, there are good reasons to keep houses that are being lived in out of the heritage domains. On the one hand, the construction of heritage is likely to adversely affect the interests and even the welfare of local populations, particularly ordinary people (cf. Herzfeld 1991). On the other hand, it also adversely affects the first life of houses as social habitats for the local populations. As such, heritage status should be accorded solely to buildings whose initial functions are already dead or extinct. Otherwise, it is necessary to reconcile the protection of cultural heritage with the people's need to live in the structure, and thereby give more importance to the social component than to the aesthetic component.

The case of Castelo Rodrigo can also be taken into account in the study of heritage (either "tangible" or "intangible"), as well as in culture theory. Here one sees clearly that we must delve beneath the surface of the cultural phenomena into the messiness of daily practices, in order to understand how things actually work out on the ground. Ethnographic case studies are not only particularly pertinent in revealing "the local specificity of a global heritage regime" (Bendix 2009: 255). They also allow us to base our theoretical discussions on strong empirical foundations and see the limitations of abstract formulations in understanding the "real world".

Notes

1 The study was made possible by a *Fundação para a Ciência e a Tecnologia* (Portuguese Foundation for Science and Technology) research grant (SFRH/BPD/34229/2006). I thank this institution for its support. I also thank the anonymous *Ethnologia Europaea* reviewer for the productive comments and suggestions on a previous version of this article. Finally, I thank the inhabitants of Castelo Rodrigo for their indispensable contribution to this study.

2 The Manueline, or Portuguese late Gothic, is the ornate Portuguese style of architecture of the first decades of the sixteenth century, incorporating maritime elements and representations of the discoveries.

3 An artefact is considered to be of "public interest"

when its protection and enhancement represent a cultural value of national importance, but for which the system of protection for "national monuments" is considered disproportionate.

4 I began to explore the case of Castelo Rodrigo in a short paper recently published (Silva 2011) but the theoretical approach here is completely different.

5 The presence of tourists in the village dates back at least to the 1970s; on March 6, 1980, the local government "decided that effort would be made to ban begging from the foreigners who visit this parish."

6 Since it opened in 2002, the tourist office has almost continuously registered a growing number of tourists annually. The historic maximum was reached in 2009 with 47,731 tourists, most of them Portuguese, followed by Spaniards due to geographical proximity; the great majority of tourists do not stay overnight in the village. With respect to supply, the local tourism industry comprises: two small tourist guesthouses, a café, a teahouse, a gourmet food store, a tourist office, and three shops selling antiques, handicrafts and local products located in the old town centre; in the outskirts, there is also a local shop, a restaurant, a camping and a leisure park with an outdoor pool.

7 The palace was built in the sixteenth century by the Marquis of Castelo Rodrigo, Cristóvão de Moura. Officially, the palace was burnt down by the inhabitants in the 1640s, after the Restoration of Portuguese Independence, because the Marquis had supported Castilian domination over the country. Explored by the municipal government, the ruin is now a pay to enter tourist attraction.

8 These two bodies disappeared in 2007 with the creation of the Institute for the Management of Architectural and Archaeological Heritage.

9 The "tourist gaze" describes the visual consumption of signs or symbols considered extraordinary from a culturally specific viewpoint and thus worthy of viewing (Urry [1990]2002). "Once people visit places outside capital cities and other major centres, what they find pleasurable are buildings which seem appropriate to a place and which mark that place off from others" (Urry 1999: 224).

10 For example, most inhabitants signed a petition against the replacement of old street lamps by modern ones, but they were not successful in achieving the purpose.

11 The village has had electricity since 1970, mains water since 1987 and sanitation since 1988.

References

Abram, S. & J. Waldren (eds.) 1998: *Anthropological Perspectives on Local Development*. London: Routledge.

Bendix, R. 2009: Heritage between Economy and Politics: An Assessment from the Perspective of Cultural Anthropology. In: L. Smith & N. Akagawa (eds.), *Intangible Heritage*. Oxon, New York: Routledge, pp. 253–269.

Bendix, R. & O. Löfgren 2008: Double Homes, Double Lives? *Ethnologia Europaea* 37:1–2, 7–15.

Bendix, R. & V. Hafstein 2009: Culture and Property: An Introduction. *Ethnologia Europaea* 39:2, 5–10.

Cavaco, C. 1995: Tourism in Portugal: Diversity, Diffusion, and Regional and Local Development. *Tijdschrift voor Economische en Sociale Geografie* 86:1, 64–71.

De Cesari, C. 2010: Creative Heritage: Palestinian Heritage NGOs and Defiant Arts of Government. *American Anthropologist* 112:4, 625–637.

Foucault, M. 1991: Governmentality. In: G. Burchell, C. Gordon & P. Miller (eds.), *The Foucault Effect: Studies in Governmentality*. Chicago: University of Chicago Press, pp. 87–104.

Foucault, M. (1994)2002: *Power (Essential Works of Foucault. 1954–1984, Vol. 3)*. J. Faubion (ed.), R. Hurley & others (trans.). London: Penguin Books.

Graham, B., G. Ashworth & J. Tunbridge 2000: *A Geography of Heritage: Power, Culture and Economy*. London: Arnold Press.

Gravari-Barbas, M. (ed.) 2005: *Habiter le patrimoine: Enjeux, approches, vécu*. Rennes: Presses Universitaires de Rennes.

Greffe, E. 1994: Is Rural Tourism a Lever for Economic and Social Development? *Journal of Sustainable Tourism* 2:1, 22–40.

Herzfeld, M. 1991: *A Place in History – Social and Monumental Time in a Cretan Town*. New Jersey: Princeton University Press.

Hodges, M. 2009: Disciplining Memory: Heritage Tourism and the Temporalisation of the Built Environment in Rural France. *International Journal of Heritage Studies* 15:1, 76–99.

Jaakson, R. 1986: Second Home Domestic Tourism. *Annals of Tourism Research* 13, 367–391.

Jenkins, J., M. Hall & M. Troughton 1998: The Restructuring of Rural Economies: Rural Tourism and Recreation as a Government Response. In: R. Butler, C. Hall & J. Jenkins (eds.), *Tourism and Recreation in Rural Areas*. Chichester: John Wiley & Sons, pp. 43–65.

Kirshenblatt-Gimblett, B. 1998: *Destination Culture: Tourism, Museums, and Heritage*. Berkeley, Los Angeles & London: University of California Press.

Leal, J. 2000: *Etnografias Portuguesas (1870–1970): Cultura Popular e Identidade Nacional*. Lisbon: Dom Quixote.

Lefebvre, H. (1972)1976: *Espacio y Política: El Derecho a la Ciudad, II*. Barcelona: Ediciones Península.

Lefebvre, H. (1974)1991: *The Production of Space*. D. Nicholson-Smith (trans.). Oxford, Malden: Blackwell.

Lindknud, C. 1998: When Opposite Worldviews Attract: A Case of Tourism and Local Development in Southern France. In: S. Abram & J. Waldren (eds.), *Anthropological*

Perspectives on Local Development. London: Routledge, pp. 141–159.

Lowenthal, D. 1985: *The Past is a Foreign Country*. Cambridge: Cambridge University Press.

Lowenthal, D. 1998: *The Heritage Crusade and the Spoils of History*. Cambridge: Cambridge University Press.

MacCannell, D. (1976)1999: *The Tourist: A New Theory of Leisure Class*. Berkeley, Los Angeles & London: University of California Press.

Macleod, D. 2010: Power, Culture and the Production of Heritage. In: D. Macleod & J. Carrier (eds.), *Tourism, Power and Culture: Anthropological Insights*. Bristol, Buffalo & Toronto: Channel View Publications, pp. 64–89.

OECD 1994: *Tourism Strategies and Rural Development*. Paris: OECD.

Rautenberg, M. 2003: *La Rupture Patrimoniale*. Paris: A la Croisée.

Rowan, Y. & U. Baram 2004: Archaeology after Nationalism: Globalization and the Consumption of the Past. In: Y. Rowan & U. Baram (eds.), *Marketing Heritage: Archaeology and the Consumption of the Past*. Walnut Creek, Calif.: Altamira Press, pp. 3–26.

Samuel, R. 1994: *Theatres of Memory. Volume 1: Past and Present in Contemporary Culture*. London & New York: Verso.

Sharpley, R. & J. Sharpley 1997: *Rural Tourism: An Introduction*. Oxford: International Thomson Business Press.

Silva, L. 2009a: *Casas no Campo: Etnografia do Turismo Rural em Portugal*. Lisbon: Imprensa de Ciências Sociais.

Silva, L. 2009b: Heritage Building in the 'Historic Villages of Portugal': Social Processes, Practices and Agents. *Journal of Ethnology and Folkloristics* 3:2, 75–91.

Silva, L. 2010: Perspectiva antropológica do turismo de habitação em Portugal. *Pasos: Revista de Turismo y Patrimonio Cultural* 8:1, 31–46, on-line http://www.pasosonline.org/Publicados/8110/PS0110_3.pdf. Accessed May 30, 2011.

Silva, L. 2011. Folk Architecture Heritagization in Rural Portugal. In: X. Roigé & J. Frigolé (eds.), *Constructing Cultural and Natural Heritage: Parks, Museums and Rural Heritage*. Girona: Institut Català de Recerca en Patrimoni Cultural, pp. 135–145.

Smith, L. 2004: *Archaeological Theory and the Politics of Cultural Heritage*. New York: Routledge.

Smith, L. 2006: *Uses of Heritage*. New York: Routledge.

Sobral, J. 2004: O *genuíno*, o *espúrio* e a identidade local: Um estudo de caso das políticas de património em meio rural. *Etnográfica* 8:2, 243–271.

Strapp, J. 1988: Resort Cycle and Second Homes. *Annals of Tourism Research* 15, 504–516.

Timothy, D. & S. Boyd 2003: *Heritage Tourism*. Harlow, Essex: Pearson Education Limited.

Tunbridge, J. & G. Ashworth 1999: *Dissonant Heritage: The Management of the Past as a Resource in Conflict*. Chichester, New York: John Wiley & Sons.

Urry, J. 1999: Gazing on History. In: D. Boswell & J. Evans (eds.), *Representing the Nation: A Reader. Histories, Heritage and Museums*. London & New York: Routledge, pp. 208–232.

Urry, J. (1990) 2002: *The Tourist Gaze*. 2nd edition. London: Sage.

Luís Silva is a post-doctoral research fellow at the Centre for Research in Anthropology, Universidade Nova de Lisboa (CRIA/FCSH-UNL). His principal research interests include rural dynamics and the anthropology of tourism, focusing specifically on the making of heritage and tourism products in rural areas, as well as on the local impact of tourism and the heritage enterprise. He has published the book *Casas no Campo: Etnografia do Turismo Rural em Portugal* (Houses in the countryside: Ethnography of rural tourism in Portugal) (Lisboa: Imprensa de Ciências Sociais, 2009).
(luis.silva98@gmail.com)

LEARNING TO EAT STRAWBERRIES IN A DISCIPLINED WAY

Normalization Practices Following Organ Transplantation

Katrin Amelang, Violetta Anastasiadou-Christophidou, Costas S. Constantinou, Anna Johansson, Susanne Lundin and Stefan Beck

This article addresses everyday strategies of coming to terms with organ transplantation that we term normalization practices. The analysis is based on focus group discussions and ethnographic interviews with transplant recipients, their relatives and waiting list patients in Sweden, Cyprus and Germany. Exploring our respondents' narratives we analytically differentiate between three levels of practices normalizing the post-transplantation experience: (1) a personal level, (2) a level of the intimate, and (3) a level of anonymous sociality. Our comparative perspective shows that sociocultural differences play a much greater role in interactive normalization practices (levels 2 and 3) than on the personal level (1), where universalized medical knowledge provides a framework that supersedes the role of cultural or social differences.

Keywords: normalization practices, chronic illness, Sweden, Cyprus, Germany

> *Well, from time to time I think about it* [the transplantation] *and I'm very grateful. But most of the time I forget about it, most likely because my liver is doing so well. Everything has become so normal already, just like before, it's hard to believe actually. I had not imagined it would turn out this good ... Of course I am still careful with my meals.* (Marlene Lukaz)[1]

Marlene Lukaz is 57 years old, lives in Berlin and received a liver transplant in 2003. To capture the meaning organ transplantation has had for her one has to go farther back in her story, beyond early 2002, when she was put on the waiting list for a new organ. At that time, she suffered from a tremendously enlarged liver full of cysts, which had developed over more than a decade and for which she had undergone painful liver punctures for many years, each puncture relieving her for a short while only. Although her polycystic liver was not life-threatening, transplantation improved her life significantly, relieving her from various burdens associated with her "*heavy belly*", which reduced her mobility, caused chronic pain and was a visual reminder of her obvious exceptionality: "*Just imagine: I appeared to be highly pregnant all the time. I couldn't even bend down to close my shoes – I never bought shoelaces. And of course my appearance stressed me psychologically. People said: look at the old bird, she is pregnant. I couldn't take it.*"

Considering all her experiences, Marlene Lukaz sees organ transplantation as a favourable medical intervention and as a success: Transplantation relieved her of suffering, considerably enhanced the way she experiences her state of health, and enabled her to look back on her chronic liver problems as a temporary, exceptional episode in her life. However, she did not return to normality in a simple, straightforward way. Instead, her everyday life is intricately shaped by the many *chronic* side-effects of transplantation: among them forced adherence to strict hygienic rules, the permanent, worrying risk of organ rejection, adverse consequences of immunosuppressive drugs, regular medical check-ups, limited capacity to work, and, as a result, her pending application for early retirement. Yet, she claims to "*forget*" about these fundamental changes in her life: She perceives neither her chronic post-transplantation condition as illness, nor her lifelong dependency on intense medical treatment as exceptional. But as the last sentence in the first quote indicates, she continuously has to intervene into her body. The treatment regime after her liver transplantation requires an active, flexible self that is capable of long-term discipline and self-governance (Rose 1998). She has to treat her body in a mode of extensive carefulness.

That Marlene Lukaz plays down the burdens of her treatment regime and instead emphasizes that she has "*a normal life*" can be interpreted as a successful coping strategy, a learned tactic: the outcome of what will be called *normalization practices* in the following. In this article, we will analyze how transplanted persons *normalize* their extraordinary condition, and we will ask how this sense of normality is achieved. Which everyday life practices and normativities are mobilized and (re)negotiated in the process?

To understand what counts as normal in the eyes of our respondents, what strategies they apply to normalize their post-transplantation situation, and which social and cultural mechanisms of in- and exclusion they have to face in doing so, our case-based analysis will explore respondents' narratives of normalization practices. Analytically we differentiate between three levels on which the post-transplantation condition is normalized: (1) a personal level, (2) a level of intimate others and family, and (3) a societal level. Drawing on a comparative perspective, we will show that sociocultural differences play a much greater role in *interactive normalization practices* (levels 2 and 3) than in *individual coping or self-normalization* (level 1), where universalized medical knowledge provides a framework that supersedes the role of cultural or social differences.

Material, Methods and Theoretical Perspectives

The following analysis draws on empirical material collected in the framework of the EU-Project "Challenges of Biomedicine: Socio-Cultural Contexts, European Governance, and Bioethics" (2004–2007).[2] The comparative project explored attitudes towards and experiences with transplantation medicine and genetic testing based on focus group discussions with patients, their relatives and laypersons, as well as ethnographic interviews with selected focus group participants.[3] This article draws on focus group and interview material from Sweden, Cyprus and Germany concerning experiences with transplantation medicine, namely the accounts of 18 transplanted persons, 5 relatives of organ recipients, one of whom donated a kidney to her husband, and 4 persons on the waiting list for an organ.[4] Despite the many social and cultural differences of the 27 participants and their different residences in Berlin, Germany (11), the region of Lund, Sweden (7), and Nicosia, Cyprus (9), central for all respondents was maintaining "a normal life", (re)gaining control over their bodies, mastering medical uncertainties, and coming to terms with the individually and socially challenging situation of living with a chronic health problem.

Normality is *the* important point of reference when respondents describe their past illness experiences and their current situations. Yet, what counts as normal is not a matter of fact but a dynamic valuation that is negotiated in specific contexts and in differentiation to what counts as abnormal (Canguilhem 2000). It implicates "how things are" just as much as "how they ought to be" (Hacking 1990:

163), ambiguously combining description and norm (cf. Therborn 2002). It is here that sociocultural difference enters the equation, since ideas about normality and abnormality are "culturally constructed and intimately associated with the social, political, and moral order" (Lock 2000: 259) of a given social context. What our respondents refer to as normal, that is, as typical, habitual, familiar or as natural, lies at the heart of anthropology's comparative inquiry of common sense(s) (Herzfeld 2001: 14). Despite its somewhat difficult reputation in anthropology, and the challenges of creating comparability of phenomena (cf. Niewöhner & Scheffer 2010; Gingrich & Fox 2002), a comparative perspective provided us with valuable insights: Cross-reading the material from the three localities provided us with valuable insights into notions and variations of what counts as normal lives with or without organ transplants in these different European localities.[5]

Anthropological research on organ transplantation emphasizes that organ recipients have to work hard for their new lives (Hauser-Schäublin et al. 2001: 175).[6] Transplantation generally is understood to be a "transformative experience" (Sharp 1995), demanding from organ recipients that they harmonize their old and new embodied selves and synchronize their subjective experiences of their modified bodies with transplantation medicine's objectified view on the body (Kalitzkus 2003). In addition, they have to "reconstruct their identities" by personally and publicly "rebuilding their sense of self" (Sharp 1995). Olivia Wiebel-Fanderl (2003) discusses individual narratives of coming to terms with transplantation as moments of biographic reconceptualisations of the self which point to individual and collective forms of coping as well as contemporary representations of transplantation medicine. We take respondents' pronouncements of how normal their lives have become after transplantation as a starting point for exploring *normalization practices* as they are embedded in different social situations and contexts of living with an organ transplant. We will examine *narratives* of normalization practices, not practices themselves – we will analyze how our respondents speak about everyday practices in a specific social and interactive setting, be it a semi-public focus group or a more intimate interview with an ethnographer. These narratives are analyzed as instances of meaning-making practices, which, most of all, serve to establish continuity with the past and an expected or desired future (Jenkins et al. 2005), and they shed light on cultural meanings and practices that surround illness experience (Kleinman 1988; Garro & Mattingly 2000).

Normalization of Chronicity as a Distributed Practice

Organ recipients may desire the normality an organ transplantation promises, but often find themselves in a state of "persistent liminality", "betwixt and between the states of 'health' and 'illness', and 'patient' (who depends on others) and 'normal person' (who participates in and contributes to a family)" (Crowley-Matoka 2005: 827).[7] In accordance with this, we analyze "transplanted 'health'" (ibid.) as a chronic health problem, in which a simple return to normality, a return to a recovered independent self as suggested in the sick-role model (Parsons 1951, 1964), is impossible. However, the Parsonian perspective on rights, obligations and reciprocities of everyday moral behaviour is nonetheless useful in understanding respondents' normalization practices as strategies of dealing with "competing expectations of an ongoing sick role and of normal everyday roles" (Varul 2010: 81). Organ recipients tend to describe the post-transplantation period as normal not in the least because any reference to problems would clash with the collective expectation that the highly costly process of organ transplantation, an important hallmark of medical progress, might have failed (cf. Mongoven 2003; Fox & Swazey 1992). Narratives of leading a normal life then can be interpreted as the outcome of a complex process aligning collective and subjective expectations of normality.

From the perspective of *health psychology*, persons with a chronic health problem have to adjust to the new situation and regulate and restore their self by reprioritizing different goals and life domains; they have to find meaning and purpose in illness experience (Sharpe & Curran 2006). Adjustment is viewed "as the process to maintain a positive view of the self and the world in the face of a health problem" (ibid.: 1161). What has to be achieved according to this perspective is a restored *psychological* equilibrium. Similarly, but focussing on *inter*acting individuals, *medical sociologists* argue that the chronically ill *and* their relatives have to develop strategies to adapt to the new situation and to neutralize their exceptional status, their deviance from the norm, through processes of normalization (Gerhardt 1990). Ideally, this is achieved by means of a biographical reconstruction of identity or by various activities that manage daily life in to being as normal as possible, e.g. covering up limitations, redefining symptoms or inventing new routines (Strauss et al. 1984; Bury 1991; Charmaz 2000). However, the chronically ill have to *react* not only as patients to dynamic processes of disease, but also to *interact* in no less dynamic social contexts: "The ability to cope is located neither wholly in individuals' personal strength nor in the condition itself. Social and material resources, life transitions and the responses of society and its institutions all impact on individual ability to cope" (Atkin & Ahmad 2001: 625). Strategies of normalizing remain thus precarious and vulnerable "to both changes in the condition, in personal and social circumstances and the disabling attitudes of others" (ibid.: 618). For that reason, illness experience in *medical anthropology* is conceptualized as "transpersonal" and "sociosomatic" (Kleinman 1988, 1997): Despite being unique and particular in its embodied subjectivity, illness experience is seen as highly embedded in social networks and life worlds, interwoven with sociocultural realities, collective patterns of meaning making and the politics of everyday life (Kleinman & Seeman 2000). Accordingly, illness experience is conceptualized as a product of complex negotiations between several social actors and cultural knowledges that are mediated through and expressed in personal accounts of perceiving, classifying and dealing with ill health and the resulting exceptionality.

Consequently, normalization cannot be adequately conceptualized as a transitory process with a (happy) endpoint of self-restoration; it is at best a rather precarious *dynamic equilibrium*, produced in a process that requires continuous, ongoing activity: a Sisyphus work. In this context, self-motivation for unrelenting (self-)interventions are a pertinent task, threatened by exhaustion, weakness, loss of motivation or the permanent threat of organ rejection. Accordingly, we conceptualize normalization in the following as a dynamic process in the making, as a process in search of a dynamic "physio-psycho-socio-cultural" equilibrium. Preconditioning this equilibrium are disciplined continuing activities and highly socially embedded practices: they routinely involve many actors, span diverse situations, and have to mobilize heterogeneous infrastructures. For this reason, we understand normalization as a *socialized, distributed practice*, involving and mobilizing personal relations. The normalization of the post-transplantation condition into *a way of life* implies a whole set of necessary normative as well as pragmatic (re)arrangements of daily (inter)actions and the negotiation of social norms and cultural expectations. Against this background, we will explore how respondents describe their medically entangled life after organ transplantation, analyze how normalizing practices unfold in this context, and finally we will examine how they deal with dependency and exceptionality. As already indicated, in the following, we will scrutinise normalization practices with respect to (1) relations to one's self, (2) relations to intimate others like families and friends, and (3) to the wider social context.

Self-Relations: Normalization of Non-Standard Bodies and Selves

Most of our respondents highlight the "*amazing*" results of transplantation and tell stories in which transplantation has been the "*last chance*" and a "*happy*" endpoint of a serious (often chronic and life-threatening) health problem. The underlying narrative plot corresponds with public presentations of transplantation stories in the media and organ donation campaigns; many tropes we encountered in these narratives are inspired by the rhetoric of transplantation medicine, depicting the substitution of organs as a technically sophisticated, but medically unproblematic fix.[8] Our respondents divide their health biographies into a time before and after transplantation, in which the time preceding transplantation is described as an exceptional episode, characterized by suffering, existential fears of organ failure and death, and the dramatic experience of waiting for an organ transplant. Whereas they mention the first days and weeks after transplantation mostly in passing, here and there illustrating the initial complications and overall hardship, they typically are quick to assure others that "*in the end everything worked out fine*". In these accounts organ recipients are more often than not depicted as suffering, passive victims depending solely on external medical intervention and altruistic donation. What is muted is their agency, their own required actions before and after transplantation surgery: In order to be put on the waiting list for an organ, potential recipients have to demonstrate to transplantation surgeons that they are willing and capable of self-intervention and that they can deal with the tough medical regime after transplantation. While respondents retell life with a transplant as a biographic turning point, they mostly play down their struggles to adapt to a self-interventionist lifestyle in their narratives. They present post-transplantation stories in which coping with their current condition becomes a normal part of daily routine that goes without saying. What is made intransparent for the outside observer are the minute self-interventions and the social resources that have to be mobilized.

Learning the Dos and the Don'ts

Organ transplantation saves lives by transforming ill health into a more liveable, yet medically dependent state. For organ recipients this means that they have to conform to a strict preventative regime. "*In the beginning that's the only thing you have on your mind*", said Yvonne Larsson from Lund, who is in her late thirties and received a lung transplant in 2003, "*but I mean – you have to live.*" After six months, she was able to "*manage a little better*" and over time learned to "*live with*" the life-long requirement of adhering to the rules. Prominent among the things our respondents permanently have to "*keep track of*" are "*pills*", "*big ones, small ones, coloured ones, all sorts of,*" that is, the immunosuppressive drugs they have to take, which weaken the immune system to prevent it from rejecting the organ transplant. The strict medication schedule (twice a day at regular intervals) has to be integrated into daily routines. For Hasan Çelik, a 47-year-old Turkish migrant who has lived in Berlin since the 1970s and who underwent liver transplantation in 1997, the intake of pills is serious work and requires the learning of new skills: "*When you're not used to it, it's hard. You'd take one after the other, and it never ends. Until I saw this woman taking them all in one go. I thought, I couldn't do it, but I tried, and it worked – it's easier that way.*" For Tobias Mårtensson in contrast, who is from Lund and had a lung transplant in 1998 because of his cystic fibrosis, the routine intake of pills was not new but a "*habit*" he had already developed before the transplantation. The self-administration of medication for him is one of many "*small things that you sort of learn to try to control* (...) just *something you have to* [do]."

The lengthy catalogue of dos and don'ts respondents listed for us can be interpreted as forms of *sub-medical* interventions into their lives. Whereas some respondents experience them as straining and as diminishing their quality of life, most consider them to be "*no problem*", easy enough to habitualize. While they play down the extent of their interventions, the "small things" they do cover the frequent and thorough washing of their hands or inquiring about the health status of guests sitting next to them at a party. There are many things to avoid, like eating raw food at a restaurant or touching the door of public buildings at the handle where most people touch it. Such seeming trivia gives a full account of how respondents integrate practices and tactics of "doing hygiene" or "doing medication" in their everyday lives. The therapeutic regime following transplantation requires of our respondents to become *active* and conscious subjects of self-interventions and self-surveillance. Rules have to be interpreted with disciplined flexibility to make them fit into daily routines or desires. Accordingly, when Marlene Lukaz – contrary to medical advice – does not give up eating strawberries, she nevertheless follows the rules of hygiene and performs a minute choreography: She examines and rinses every single fruit properly, eats them one after the other, and in case one of them tastes slightly rotten, spits it out and washes her mouth before performing the same procedure on the next one.

Apart from one's home becoming a location of therapeutic self-intervention, respondents regularly have to attend medical check-ups in which particularly the function of the transplanted organ is examined, in order to exclude the imminent danger of organ rejection. When respondents jokingly state that they are "*married*" to their doctors or hospitals, they refer to the frequent routine of their visits and the implicated rules of engagements with their doctors. Compliance with the treatment regime and medical knowledge play a central and unquestioned role in the lives of all our respondents. Yet, individual physicians are rarely mentioned in the Swedish and German respondents' accounts, instead, medical expertise appears in a generalized and impersonal mode expressed in phrases like "it's just – one cannot …" or "the only thing is – I shouldn't..." Interestingly, individual doctors figure prominently in Cypriot narratives. We take this presence or absence of references as an indicator of the degree to which the physician's guidance is not taken as resulting from a *personal*, but from a *professional* relationship; in the latter case, the individual physician disappears behind a corpus of abstract expertise. Accordingly, the treatment regimen is presented and experienced by our German and Swedish respondents as generalized rules which have to be accepted and eventually become habitualized as a rather unquestioned part of daily, bodily routine. Cypriot respondents, however, rely on *and* expect modes of guidance that are more personal.

Generally, respondents have to deal with abstract values, data and figures that survey, monitor and measure their bodily functions. These "objective", medical observational techniques increasingly displace normal, unaided modes of introspection – "*listening to one's body*" will not do, as Regine Paulitz, a German participant who had a heart transplanted, put it: "*You have to let them* [physicians] *look at you all the time, because I can't look inside myself.*" Since organ rejection cannot be felt by ordinary senses, respondents experience the feeling of losing control: they have to subject themselves to objective medical observation and have to rely on objectified medical facts and interpretations. This erosion of the ability to trust in subjective, circumstantial self-experience is perceived by our respondents as a fundamental shift in the way they experience their bodies. They have to adopt a new mode of reflexivity, learning to perceive themselves and their state of well-being through for instance blood parameters. Having learned the numerous lessons of self-objectification, respondents develop a remarkable mode of objectified reflexivity. They become experts in interpreting medical data and learn to infer how they are and how they feel through the interpretation of medical data. In these iterative "looping processes" (Hacking 2006) – from subject to object and subject again – they learn to trust in a technologically extended mode of self-perception. These self-techniques demand a self-controlling subjectivity that is already selected for *before* transplantation: As Yvonne Larsson put it, "*I don't get a transplant if they* [physicians] *think I can't handle it.*"

Overall, the therapy regime following organ transplantation structures the activities of our respondents in an intricate way, establishing a tight temporal-spatial grid and a highly disciplined individual. Medicine offers a strong framework that requires individual regularity and routinization as well as a new mode of self experience. Medical knowledge of organs, immune systems and the effects of immunosuppression is incorporated into everyday knowledge. Preventative practices after organ transplantation are based on a highly normalized – in the sense of a normative as well as unquestioned – choreography of temporal, spatial and social settings. Thus, the required self-interventions of health management become normal parts of everyday routines.

Accepting and Growing into Exceptionality

What a chronic health problem is and means is learnt the hard way: "Lessons in chronicity come in small everyday experiences" (Charmaz 2000: 282). All our respondents had to and "*did grow into* [illness] *little by little*," and thus into a condition that finally resulted in transplantation. Equally gradual was the escalation of medical interventions set in motion by the first diagnosis. Retrospectively, several respondents describe that the step-by-step procedure of medical intervention and the subdivision of health problems into smaller units of medically manageable subproblems reduced fear; seeing not the "*whole process*" but rather only the "*next step*" tended to reduce fear. For many respondents the option of transplantation appeared less disturbing, particularly since a partiality of knowledge or even partial ignorance was perceived as reassuring. Exemplary is a statement of Sotiris Georgiou, a 63-year-old Cypriot who received a kidney from his wife, when he discusses the case of an acquaintance who lost her kidney due to a rejection and had to undergo retransplantation: "*It is harder than the first time or when under haemodialysis because during haemodialysis the person does not really know. The second time, he/she knows both situations and is afraid to go back and have the transplantation again.*"

He interprets his own health biography in terms of destiny: "*In my opinion, God gives us the opportunity to go through hardship in order to come closer to him.*" Similarly, Anna Kyriakou, a 19-year-old from Nicosia who had bone marrow transplantation, states: "*Of course, I asked where this disease* [leukaemia] *comes from and even physicians told us they do not know, and therefore I took it as a sent sufferance.*" Here, illness-experience is normalized by integrating it into cosmological understandings and beliefs: individual suffering is understood as destiny or as sent from God. Interpreted in the framework of religion, illness appears to be normal or at least purposive, and personal coping with illness is transformed into a religious obligation. The role of medicine is to help deal with the consequences but it certainly does not provide sufficient explanation and support. Respondents, who present themselves explicitly as non-religious, also employ images of destiny. Many respondents use medical and non-medical explanations simultaneously to embed illness in everyday cosmologies about life, because medical knowledge provides explanations that regularly fail to address questions of individual suffering.

"*To face life as it comes*" is an often used expression by respondents that seems to unveil a fatalist attitude but rather refers to active processes of ideational self-intervention: our respondents aim at redefining the meaning of illness and (post)transplantation experience as positive. In this regard, a Cypriot focus group participant who needs haemodialysis and is currently on a waiting list for a kidney says: "*My experience made me unafraid to live with the problem, and I tell everybody who has haemodialysis to befriend it in order to be able to deal with it.*" Getting used to going through haemodialysis regularly in his case is the result of accepting and creating a "friendship" with the process: he adapts to his situation by redefining it.

Generally, respondents state how important it is to adopt a *positive attitude*. The implementation of positive thinking involves the process of coming to terms with the chronicity of one's health condition and accepting limited capacities. For many respondents this meant discarding the ideal self-image of healthy normality and taking an approach that emphasizes what they still can do. They implicitly contrast their own positions to attitudes of self-pity, passivity and feelings of capitulation, in order to reframe their coping strategies as good practice. For many respondents, good practice includes self-empowerment by acquiring knowledge and information of their health problem and transplantation. They view medical statistics as well as experiences of other organ recipients as helpful sources for facing their situation in an informed manner. These approaches entail a normative notion of how one should cope with transplantation and correspond to current images of successful ways of dealing with health problems which Cameron Hay identified for the U.S. context as a "culturally legitimated John-Wayne-model" (Hay 2010) where health problems are conceptualized as failure to take care of oneself (Greco 1993). The mastering of health in a continuous process of self-intervention thus becomes an obligation. In this sense, ideational self-interventions add to the practical activities with which our respondents take care of themselves. Usually these self-interventions are naturalized by our respondents by grounding them in their own personalities, instead of attributing them to painfully learned practices.

Two Modes of Normalization

On a more abstract level we found two different modes of normalization based on underlying rationalities. First, there is the mode of *adapting* life through practical activities that restructure everyday routines in accordance with the treatment regime following organ transplantation. Here, *praxeologies* dominate that are mainly guided by medical discourses. In contrast, the second mode of normalization practices is exemplified by practices of *retelling* or *reconceptualizing* life. Here, *ideologies* dominate redefinitions or re-evaluations of self-images and self-understandings against the backdrop of commonsensical, vernacular normativities or aesthetic judgements. Both modes of normalization then, are intensely socialized and closely interwoven with and dependent on pre-existing sociotechnical infrastructures which act and give meaning to actions. The discourse of medicine, its vocabulary and technologies as well as its truth claims are central mediators (Beck 2007) for both strategies. Our respondents use medical knowledges and techniques as a powerful repository to integrate illness experience into everyday routines, to de-exeptionalize their respective conditions and to create new modes of self-relation, self-knowledge, self-reflection and self-representation.

Despite our respondents' different health problems, their biographies and strategies of restructuring life before and after organ transplantation, and their struggle to adapt life follow a common pattern. All of them are confronted with therapeutic interventions and treatment regimes of transplantation medicine's follow-up care that are characterized by a large degree of standardization across Europe.[9] Accordingly, they mobilize equally uniform self-interventions; as a result, respondents in Sweden, Cyprus and Germany pursue highly similar adapting strategies. More variation becomes apparent when we shift the focus from medical dominated self-interventions to the mode of retelling life under the new conditions of being chronically ill. Yet overall, these kinds of normalization practices appear to follow common patterns, too, leaving little space for cultural differences. Beyond these generalizations, respondents' stories mirror the manifold individual competencies and sociocultural resources on which they can draw. These resources can be religious beliefs, practices, education and lifestyle orientations, prior experiences with illness or befriended doctors. What our material shows is that self-interventions refer to ways in which individuals recognise themselves, redefine ideas of (ab)normality and in the end position themselves in the shifting poles of being both normal and exceptional. However, the self-interventions we have described so far are only understood adequately if they are interpreted as highly embedded, socialized and cultured practices that unfold in interactions with others. This contextuality is even more relevant for normalization practices on the level of respondents' relation with intimate others.

Relations to Intimate Others: Familial Normalization and Mutual Obligations

In addition to the individualized mode of adapting to the chronic health condition after transplantation, chronic health problems and ways of dealing with them require an interactive mode since relations to intimate others – the partner, relatives, or close friends – are substantially affected. These intimate others experience illness and transplantation as outsiders but regularly share the hopes and sorrows of their loved ones. Studies of the family setting within which chronic illness is dealt with show that the quality of family relationships strongly influences how disruptive the illness is experienced to be (Gregory 2005: 382). The transformations caused by illness, necessary therapeutic activities, acceptance of exceptionality or the redefinition of self-images affect ill individuals as well as their intimate others and have to be integrated into family relations (Corbin & Strauss 1988). Being "both unexpected and unwelcome," serious illness and chronic health problems "can test the fabric of normal family life" (Gregory 2005: 376).

Redefined Relationships

Without being affected themselves, the consequences of serious illness and transplantation affect the lives of those who accompany and support transplanted respondents during the uncertain process. This becomes apparent in the term "we" one Swedish focus group participant uses to refer to the shared experiences of hope and uncertainty when her husband was on the waiting list for a lung transplant: "*When we were on the list, well we – you become* (...), *it affects the whole family.*" Since the whole family is influenced, experience of illness to a certain degree is collective. On the other hand, transplanted respondents often state that their family members are not fully able to understand their illness since they are not sharing the bodily experience. This does not necessarily involve *a lack* of experience but refers to differing perspectives of the same situation. Hasan Çelik, for example, contrasts his and his wife's experience of transplantation: While he simply "*woke up*" after surgery, his wife experienced the long hours a liver transplantation takes with all its uncertainty and anxiety. Most transplanted respondents and relatives of organ recipients alike experience illness and transplantation as intensifying mutual relations. This is typically expressed as "*getting closer to each other*" or as a new acknowledgment of "*appreciating things*". Many respondents report a fundamental change in attitudes towards life and a reprioritization of goals in favour of non-materialist interests, spending more time with family and friends or trying to improve relationships with them.

However, several respondents mentioned that reactions of close companions can also be an obstacle on the way to normalization. Family members, more often than not, are described as hampering normalization by "*worrying too much*" or by displaying *too much* concern about the ill family members' health condition, especially after organ transplantation. As a result, some respondents note that they do not always tell their family members when their condition worsens or they experience a little crisis. One 32-year-old German respondent distinguishes between her parents and her friends, indicating that the latter rather support normalization, for example, when going with her to a bar and gossiping all night, thus engaging with her in the normal activities persons of her age do, despite her health problem. Altogether, intimate others hold an ambivalent position in respondents' accounts as both saboteurs and supporters of the patients' attempts to normalize their condition. Although respondents consider their close associates overall as supportive and helpful, they hardly ever mention the daily support given and the contribution to the daily needs of coping. Similarly, they often leave implicit the material and practical consequences of illness that might affect other family members. An exception is Anna Kyriakou who had to go to Great Britain for her bone marrow transplantation; she reflects about the grave costs for her parents. She was afraid that her illness would disrupt her social life (having to leave school) as well as the social lives of her parents: "*I was thinking about my parents and that they would come with me for six months, and have to leave their jobs. Where would they find money again etc. – they would lose their jobs.*"

Intimate others of transplanted patients care and take care; that they do so is mostly taken for granted. What is often described as "*coming together in the face of serious illness*" is perceived as normal by most of our respondents. This kind of taken-for-grantedness becomes especially apparent in the extreme case of 50-year-old Andreas Moyseos from Nicosia who is on haemodialysis and has been waiting for a kidney transplant for several years. His mother had been identified as a potential donor but in the end she opted out and did not proceed with donating one of her kidneys to her son, a change of mind he could not comprehend: "*After what happened to me and how close relatives and especially my so-called mother treated me, I believed that there was no humanitarism. I was very disappointed, and I saw the world in black. I considered them all to be Judas – traitors.*" For him, his mother did not fulfil her natural obligations as she declined to sacrifice her health for her son.[10] Re-defining her as not his "real" mother makes his experience more acceptable in a society where the mother-child relation is expected to be strong and unbreakable.

Challenging Moral Economies in Intimate Relations

Moral *cum* economic obligations within the family are a central subject for transplanted respondents, particularly when it comes to their own obligations. They particularly address role expectations of being a good partner and a regular contributor to family life as they are challenged by illness and transplantation. In this regard, Paul Meyer, a German in his late fifties who underwent heart transplantation twice, argues that "*it is not so surprising that so many women leave their heart transplanted husbands*" since they cannot offer "*certain things*" any longer. Health problems, bodily condition and side effects of immunosuppressive drugs may reduce earning capacities as well as "*libido*". After transplantation, he had to give up his leading position in a company and for several years now relies on a small pension, a minijob, and the income of his wife. His reduced socioeconomic position in his family conflicts with dominant images of masculinity, his aspiration to be "*head of the family*", as well as his self-image of being a "*good husband*" and the principal provider of family income. The altered sexual relation to his wife adds to the obstacles of his struggle to live up to his expectations. His efforts to cope with his new dependencies point to the redefinition of marital and gender relations that chronic illness might initiate. Moreover, it indicates unmet expectations that "things will become normal" after transplantation. The time and effort needed to adapt to the transformation from independent income provider to dependent early retiree is a topic of both female and male respondents.

Before and after organ transplantation respondents depend on different degrees of care and support from their families, a challenge to their sense of autonomy. Especially the Swedish and German respondents talk openly about their worries with respect to reduced working and earning capacities. However, these topics do not appear equally prominent in our Cypriot material. We do not interpret this as an *absence of problems*, but rather as the outcome of *different sociocultural constellations* and of the different histories and functions of the respective welfare systems. More specifically, we interpret these results as the consequence of a dialectical process where welfare systems tend to individualize subjects by providing the chronically ill patient with a reliable, if small, source of income, as is the case in Sweden and Germany. Here the welfare state, and not family and the wider kinship network, is supposed to provide for the basic needs of the individual. In contrast, the Cypriot material suggests that extended families (Argyrou 1996) and peer groups are the most dominant and stable form of solidarity, at least concerning health care. In addition, family relations in Sweden and Germany tend to depend much more on the (re)negotiation of the family roles of the partners: traditional role models are challenged by many processes, for example in the economic, legal, social and cultural domains. As Viviana A. Zelizer (2005) convincingly shows in an analysis of similar processes in U.S.-American family life, family members have to *actively* negotiate how moral, immaterial, material and economic resources are utilized and exchanged, since traditional models are increasingly inadequate with lifestyles in a neoliberal setting.

More often than not, respondents discuss the issue of dependency only in terms of medical dependencies, or dependency on welfare and societal solidarity rather than in terms of dependencies on family members. How is it to be explained, that although our respondents briefly mention activities of family members and friends that support them, they mostly leave out the many activities concerning the self-management of disease which often become a matter of family management? On the one hand, this can be explained as a result of an ethnographic effect of the focus group and interview questions: We asked individuals, not families, how they cope with transplantation, enhancing a methodological individualism. On the other hand, this partial silence might also result from the fact that mutual obligations are taken for granted in families in all domains of social life, but especially in the face of grave existential threats. Additionally, many of the required self-interventions our respondents have to perform are related to gendered divisions of labour within families, for example taking consideration of strict hygienic rules and preparing meals. To put it differently, familial solidarity is *tacitly* taken for granted and becomes topical for respondents only in the rare case when familial solidarity is challenged – as in the case of Andreas Moyseos mentioned above. As became obvious even from the rare instances where respondents made the family involvement topical, a perspective that considers the familial context as central for normalization practices after transplantation is inevitable. Accordingly, a departure from the individualistic bias in the treatment regimes of transplantation medicine is necessary. As a Cypriot focus group participant put it: "[The] *environment plays a role in the course of* [disease]. *Where you live and the support you have play a role. I believe in this more than I believe in medicine.*" In the following, we will provide some insights into how our respondents perceive of normalization in their social environments beyond their families.

Social Relations and Interactions

Above, we have conceptualized normalization as a relational process in the dynamic social constellations of the family. To achieve a sense of normality at the workplace or even in anonymous social environments involves many more contingencies and complexities for our respondents. Strategies of normalization outside of the close circle of intimate persons are to a certain extent in other people's hands. In the following, we will take up respondents' normalization strategies with respect to (1) social norms and stigmatization, (2) obligations of being a productive member of society, and (3) self-help groups as new forms of collective solidarity.

Confronting Stigmatization

Respondents frequently feel that they depend on other people's opinion, understanding or positive evaluation when they try to normalize their health problems; and they experience these dependencies in quite a diverse manner. Of special concern are those interactions with anonymous others when there is no opportunity to explain one's exceptionality and where stigmatization and prejudice have to be confronted. How individuals deal with stigmatization depends on the stigmatizing attributes and on the visibility of one's otherness (cf. Goffman 1963). Marlene Lukaz, whom we quoted in the beginning of this paper, suffered because of her "*big belly*" which made her stand out. For her, transplantation ended not only her yearlong suffering but also her exceptional appearance. For Anna Kyriakou, in contrast, transplantation resulted in her stigmatization because she lost her hair. She recalls an instance where she walked down Makarios Street, the most popular street in the centre of Nicosia, full of shops and cafeterias. When she was passing one of the cafés, someone sitting there commented on her hair and looks, whereupon others questioned whether she was "*a boy or a girl*". For the 19-year-old, this short encounter was devastating. Makarios Street can be likened to a catwalk where pedestrians as well as drivers are subjected to anatomical, moral, economic and cultural inspection. For women of Anna's age, a perfect body in this setting means to command *the* most important capital. That her peer group, men of her age and potential marriage candidates, were making fun of her was truly painful and frustrating to her.

Apart from Anna Kyriakou's case, respondents' references to stigmatization experiences primarily concern the time before organ transplantation. What is visible afterwards are transplantation scars, which often can be hidden, and in some cases side effects of immunosuppression like tremors or a "moon face". Not surprisingly, it is mostly our female respondents who refer to such visible aspects of their condition which provoke hard to ignore looks and comments for contravening social norms that still apply more strictly to women (cf. Saltonstall 1993; Biordi 2009). But our male respondents also wonder what impression others might get when confronted with their preventative practices. Hasan Çelik, for example, refers to the strict hygienic precautions he keeps up: "*That is something – to people who don't know me I might appear – 'Jesus, he's so fussy!' I've internalized it. Hygiene is on top.*" Such examples show that our respondents have a keen understanding of social norms and the play of social power relations involved in stigmatizing comments. Åke Lindgren, a heart-transplant recipient in his fifties from Lund, brings in a different perspective on the matter of judging others: "*I guess I dissociated myself from* [handicapped] *people before* [transplantation] (...) *It's completely different today.*" He relates this change in attitudes to the new values or a new perspective on life that he, like other respondents, claims to have developed after going through severe illness experience.

Whether respondents are able to cope with offending judgements of others depends on the social situations and constellations as well as of the position respondents have in social hierarchies. Nevertheless, the ability to prevent disclosure of one's non-conformity can be understood as an important aspect of self-determination when coming to terms with illness and transplantation. Regarding the three different locations where our respondents live, we observed that in the small society of the Republic of Cyprus, the range of variation in what counts as normal or not is rather small and thus the pressure for respondents to conform is higher. However, the invisibility of health problems can be a burden too, since visibility affords opportunities for social recognition and legitimation of difference: "[P]eople who are unable to engage in everyday work, self-care, and social activity experience invisibility as a serious handicap" (Hay 2010: 267).

Working One's Way Back into Society

When respondents talk about personal and social consequences of illness and transplantation, references to personal careers are prominent. The possibility to return to work after transplantation, or to work despite being bodily and energetically restricted, is for many respondents a central means of normalization. Work can keep one busy when being on the waiting list or enables one to preserve a domain of life unchanged and normal. The ability to work and to earn a living fundamentally influences our respondents' self-images, their sense of autonomy and secures their familiar roles in their families. Moreover, even partial economic independence defines relationships to systems of social solidarity in a specific way: Those who work pay taxes or social security dues, those who contribute to the national social security system do not feel completely dependent. Åke Lindgren perceives the return to work as a means of individual normalization but he interestingly does so in the framework of social values: After transplantation "*the demands come back, you have to be moulded into society, you have to get back to it.*" One needs rehabilitation and "*energy*" but in the end, "*that's the point of it all, going back to a job.*" "To be moulded (back) into society" expresses in a strong metaphor the desire to return to being a normal, fully respected member of society. Living up to this demand requires self-intervention, yet, when Åke Lindgren started work training six months after his heart transplantation, he soon experienced the new limits of his capacities – working part-time was the new limit of what he could take. In addition, his attitude towards the relation of work and life had changed: "*Life comes first* [now]." Before his heart attack and transplantation, work came first. He describes himself as a career-oriented person who always worked a lot, a habit which took its toll, as he states. Nonetheless, he stresses the importance of going back to work to prevent what he views an illness identity. To support his claim, he contrasts his situation with that of an acquaintance who underwent heart transplantation at the same time he did. He describes this man as one of those persons "*who live in their illness,*" someone who "*lives in his transplantation role*" and, although he manages well and lives a decent life free of complications, he "*is nothing but a heart transplant recipient,*" someone who "*hasn't gotten himself a life afterwards.*" More specifically, his acquaintance "*had a problem getting back into the labour market*" and thus "*ended up standing outside.*" His acquaintance fails in Åke Lindgren's eyes because he does not make himself useful to society again and evades social demands. What he does not take into account, but what some of our respondents experienced the hard way, is the simple fact that it is not necessarily his acquaintance's fault that the labour market is apparently not giving him a second chance. Like other respondents, Åke Lindgren emphasizes work as one of the main factors which contributes to the individual's well-being and which is a prerequisite to really being a part of society. His statements show how strongly social norms influence modes of rendering life as normal.

Forms of Organizing Solidarity

A specific social form of organizing self-interventions and solidarity that relates to both the individual and the social levels, are patient groups. Here, respondents interact with like-minded or equally concerned persons and share the experience of understanding and managing a specific health problem and medical intervention (cf. Rabinow 1999; Kaufert 1998). Medical information, addresses of "good" physicians, but predominantly patients' problems and experiences are shared in these groups – including experiential knowledge of how illness feels and tips for doing post-transplantation management. Several of our respondents think these support groups are as valuable as medical information provided in the clinics: whereas their physicians have no direct bodily experiences of the conditions they treat, here patients can tap into the direct experiences and understandings of fellow sufferers. In this sense, self-help groups have an important mediating function for both the medical system and patients. Taking place in hospitals, private houses, Internet forums, electronic or paper versions of magazines, these exchanges take on different forms of social communication. Respondents who are members of patient groups state that their participation supported their learning process and thus helped with normalization. Several of them learned for example that an organ rejection is not an abstract risk but is normal rather than exceptional. In order to normalize the risk and the occurrence of a rejection episode they mobilized different knowledges – of other patients or medical statistics. In such examples, patient groups provide a collective frame of sameness and a valuable instrument that allows the de-exceptionalization of one's experience. Meeting patients who are in a better or worse condition than oneself, provides a comparative perspective that might be helpful for individual patients – a function largely unexplored in psychological studies (Dibb & Yardley 2006).

Self-help groups provide a normative framework and create an atmosphere where techniques of self-intervention are highly valued, a mind-set which might appeal only to a segment of patients, excluding others (cf. Schmidtgunst 2005). Moreover, patient groups often combine internal activities of self-help and external initiatives like public relations and lobbying. When acting in the public sphere and making transplant recipients' concerns and interests public, patient groups utilize strategies of both normalization and exceptionalization. When engaging in public campaigns in favour of organ donation, they usually stress the normality of organ transplantation and present themselves as living examples of medical success and a restored normality. Complications, ambivalences or necessary self-interventions are again muted. When respondents or patient groups lobby for financial support from the state or the healthcare system in order to maintain their place at work, or when they engage in public discussions about changes in transplantation law, they in contrast use strategies of self-othering and emphasize their exceptionality in order to receive attention.

Yet, going public can also be viewed as an expression of normalization from an individual perspective. Anna Kyriakou, for instance, talks openly about her experiences with leukaemia and bone marrow transplantation at public events or in schools in order to function as a "*vivid example*" and "*inform*" and "*sensitize*" people about the issues at stake. This can be interpreted at two levels: First, she successfully underwent transplantation and can now live a normal live – in a sense, her life is normal as it is. Second, her normalized life helps her to accept her experience and helps other people to do the same. Altogether, membership in patient groups offers flexible possibilities for making sense of illness experience and relates to concepts of both normalization and exceptionalization. More ambiguous is what respondents do with this duality of instruments provided. Our material suggests that there are two rather oppositional approaches to this: There are several respondents who participate in patient groups and for whom membership provides security, group identity and thus normalization in the sense of experiencing sameness. But there are many more respondents for whom *not* participating – keeping a distance from fellow sufferers – indicates successful normalization.

Conclusion

Scrutinizing how transplant recipients in Cyprus, Germany, and Sweden normalize their extraordinary condition and achieve what they call a normal life we have analyzed respondents' narratives of normalization practices on three levels of (inter-)action: differentiating between individual/self-related, familial and social practices of normalization. Differences between the three locations are more apparent on a meso- or macro-level, in relation to family, co-workers, or the welfare system than on the level of the individual; here the strict guidance of medical therapy regimes is dominant. The constant threat of loosing the organ through rejection especially defines the limit of normalization for all our respondents and enforces an adherence to the medical regime and a highly disciplined way of life. Our respondents are simultaneously patients, who depend on advanced medical intervention and learn to see and feel their bodies mediated through the medical gaze, as well as normal participants of ongoing daily life (cf. Crowley-Matoka 2005). They have to reconcile these conflicting roles and expectations; most of them – as we have shown – do so quite successfully. In this regard, the two modes of normalization practices we have analyzed on the individual level – the adapting and retelling of life – as well as the analyzed rearrangements of familial and social relations attest to successful strategies of coming to terms with their condition after organ transplantation as a normal way of life. *On the one hand*, these normalization practices can be interpreted as ongoing attempts to stabilize their biographies and everyday lives in the midst of health-related uncertainties. For most of them, "sickness has become a way of life" (Stacey 1988: 143). But what is normal and routine is not an unproblematic given: Normalization understood as the long and sometimes painful process of producing normality means coming to terms with being exceptional, doing exceptional things – like taking unusual amounts of medication, taking hygienic precautions, legitimizing otherness in diverse social contexts as well as being dependent on regular monitoring by medical experts. In this regard, biographical, cultural and social differences between our respondents are rather limited: Their actions are embedded in a medical praxeology. *On the other hand*, coping with transplantation is not restricted to the adherence to medical treatment regimes. Instead, it means negotiating relations with intimate or anonymous others about obligations, confronting stigmatization, and being disabled in certain aspects. It further means that transplanted persons have to reconceptualize their biographies and aspirations. In this regard, different cultural cosmologies, diverse social settings, as well as the way in which the medical system or the welfare state provides support, play a crucial role in affording an opportunity structure for transplant recipients which they can use for normalizing their lives.

The important role that the social environment plays in normalization goes beyond the current scope of this study that is based on the analysis of patients' narratives. A more thorough investigation of modes of normalization concerning our respondents' relations and interactions in a wider social context would require the observation of actual practices, hence: an ethnographic account based on participant observation. Only such a mode of inquiry could reveal how normalization strategies unfold in clinical contexts or family settings or social situations by negotiating the dynamics of everyday post-transplantation life-in-practice. To capture the complex dynamics of normalization on the level of everyday practices more systematically and to render our explorative insights more feasible, further ethnographic research is needed.[11] Such kind of research should follow organ recipients more closely during the (post)transplantation process and its different challenges to normalization. In addition to such ethnographic case studies, a more elaborate comparative approach (as opposed to the explorative one used in the context of this research) could provide further insights into the subtleties of culture at work in normalization practices. Particularly our finding that cultural differences appear to be marginal at the level of self-related normalization practices concerning the medical treatment regime, asks for clarification regarding the question of how these findings relate to recent studies in medical anthropology and science studies that emphasize the local situatedness of medical practices. While we assumed – based on the accounts of our respondents – that clinical practices, medical knowledge provided, and interventions of physicians followed internationally established best practices a closer look at local differences might be highly enlightening. As we hope to have shown, a research interest in normalization practices could bridge the special interests of medical anthropology, a growing attention towards local differences in the functioning of "medical platforms" (Keating & Cambrosio 2000) and the general anthropological interest in everyday life practices and local understandings of normality or normativity.

Notes

1 Names used for research participants are pseudonyms, all quotes from empirical material are italicized.

2 Project no. SAS6-CT-2003-510238, details available at: http://www.univie.ac.at/virusss/cobpublication; for a summary of ethnographic findings in Sweden, Germany and Cyprus, cf. Beck et al. (2006).

3 Participants were recruited via public flyers, key persons and the snowball system, hospitals, and patient associations, and were selected to be preferably diverse and balanced regarding criteria such as gender, age, education and religion. Regarding the latter less variety existed: Swedish participants were mostly Protestant and all Cypriot respondents were Greek Cypriots and Christian Orthodox. The variety in the kinds of transplants – in Lund (heart, lung), in Nicosia (kidney, bone marrow), in Berlin (heart, kidney, liver) – depended on locally present transplant centres. All transplanted participants got at least through the first two years of living with a transplant and they represent the rather successful, i.e. unproblematic, cases of transplantation.

4 Additionally, we could rely on previous ethnographic work and research carried out in the three countries by the respective teams, concerning transplantation medicine and biotechnology (Lundin), genetic testing, bone marrow transplantation and cross-cultural analysis (Beck), and the impact of medical/genetic knowledge and social aspects of health and disease on notions of solidarity and bodily integrity (Anastasiadou-Christophidou).

5 For a more detailed consideration of the usage of comparison in the project, which was undertaken as an epistemic practice by researchers and research participants likewise, cf. Amelang & Beck (2010).

6 For ethnographic analyses of the ways in which individuals and societies deal with transplantation medicine's usage of human body material and its prerequisite of the donor's brain death, see e.g. Fox & Swazey (1992), Hogle (1999) and Lock (2002). On the rhetoric of donation and altruism legitimizing the societal access of individual bodies in organ donation, see e.g. Ohnuki-Tierny (1994), Strathern (1997) and Lock & Crowley-Matoka (2008).

7 This "being in-between" applies to chronically ill persons in general, who are in medical terms confronted with a long-lasting or recurrent abnormality of the body causing discomfort or severe suffering and whose actual state of well-being as well as previous meanings, self-conceptions and ways of living are challenged considerably (Bury 1982; Charmaz 1991; Corbin & Strauss 1988).

8 Lundin's research (2002) examines the cultural processes which embed biotechnological interventions such as xenotransplantation into everyday life and thus rework what is threatening into what is familiar.

9 The differences in the implementation of care for transplanted patients as well as contrasts in the institutional contexts of medical care or distinctions in the sociocultural contexts of health policies between Sweden, Germany and Cyprus cannot be taken into account here in a systematic fashion. For further information, cf. Beck et al. (2006).

10 To prevent organ trade, living donation is allowed between relatives and emotionally close associates only. Voluntariness is the key principle but neglects, as the case of Andreas Moyseos indicates, the (pressure of) moral obligations within familial and close relationships.

11 Two in-depth studies in this regard are (1) Costas S. Constantinou's ethnographic study of kidney transplantation in Cyprus (2009) in which he examines the reconstruction of normality with respect to the mechanisms through which the experience of haemodialysis and kidney transplantation as well as the social context in which it occurs is dynamically constructed; and (2) the nearly completed dissertation of Katrin Amelang, in which she tackles the anthropologically self-evident categories of everyday life and normality by scrutinizing how liver-transplant recipients and health professionals in Germany pick out everyday routinization and normalization as a central theme.

References

Amelang, K. & S. Beck 2010: Comparison in the Wild and more Disciplined Usages of an Epistemic Practice. In: T. Scheffer & J. Niewöhner (eds.), *Thick Comparison:*

Reviving the Ethnographic Aspiration. Leiden: Brill, pp. 155–179.

Argyrou, V. 1996: *Tradition and Modernity in the Mediterranean: The Wedding as Symbolic Struggle*. Cambridge: Cambridge University Press.

Atkin, K. & W.I. Ahmad 2001: Living a 'Normal' Life: Young People Coping with Thalassaemia Major or Sickle Cell Disorder. *Social Science & Medicine* 53:5, 615–626.

Beck, S. 2007: Medicalizing Culture(s) or Culturalizing Medicine(s). In: R.V. Burri & J. Dumit (eds.), *Biomedicine as Culture*. London: Routledge, pp. 17–33.

Beck, S. et al. 2006: Short Report on Selective Interviews. Deliverable no. 3 of the EU-Project "Challenges of Biomedicine." Available as pdf at: www.euroethno.hu-berlin.de/forschung/projekte/abgeschlossene/challenges/. Accessed July 5, 2011.

Biordi, D. 2009: Body Image. In: P.D. Larsen & I.M. Lubkin (eds.), *Chronic Illness: Impact and Intervention*. 7th edition. Sudbury: Jones and Bartlett, pp. 117–137.

Bury, M. 1982: Chronic Illness as Biographical Disruption. *Sociology of Health & Illness* 4:2, 167–182.

Bury, M. 1991: The Sociology of Chronic Illness: A Review of Research and Prospects. *Sociology of Health & Illness* 13:4, 451–468.

Canguilhem, G. 2000: The Normal and the Pathological. In: F. Delaporte (ed.), *A Vital Rationalist: Selected Writings from Georges Canguilhem*. New York: Zone Books, pp. 321–350.

Charmaz, K. 1991: *Good Days, Bad Days: The Self in Chronic Illness and Time*. New Brunswick: Rutgers University Press.

Charmaz, K. 2000: Experiencing Chronic Illness. In: G.L. Albrecht et al. (eds.), *Handbook of Social Studies in Health & Medicine*. London: Sage, pp. 277–292.

Constantinou, C.S. 2009: Transplanted Selves: Kidney Transplantation in Cyprus and the Reconstruction of Normality. Dissertation. University of Bristol: Department of Archaeology and Anthropology.

Corbin, J.M. & A.L. Strauss 1988: *Unending Work and Care*. San Francisco: Jossey-Bass.

Crowley-Matoka, M. 2005: Desperately Seeing 'Normal': The Promises and Perils of Living with Kidney Transplantation. *Social Science & Medicine* 61:4, 821–831.

Dibb, B. & L. Yardley 2006: How Does Social Comparison within a Self-Help Group Influence Adjustment to Chronic Illness? A Longitudinal Study. *Social Science & Medicine* 63:6, 1602–1613.

Fox, R.C. & J.P. Swazey 1992: *Spare Parts: Organ Replacement in American Society*. New York: Oxford University Press.

Garro, L.C. & C. Mattingly 2000: Narrative as Construct and Construction. In: C. Mattingly & L.C. Garro (eds.), *Narrative and the Cultural Construction of Illness and Healing*. Berkeley: University of California Press, pp. 1–49.

Gerhardt, U. 1990: Introductory Essay. Qualitative Research on Chronic Illness: The Issue and the Story. *Social Science & Medicine* 30:11, 1149–1159.

Gingrich, A. & R.G. Fox (eds.) 2002: *Anthropology, by Comparison*. London: Routledge.

Goffman, E. 1963: *Stigma: Notes on the Management of Spoiled Identity*. New York: Simon & Schuster.

Greco, M. 1993: Psychosomatic Subjects and the 'Duty to be Well': Personal Agency within Medical Rationality. *Economy and Society* 22:3, 357–372.

Gregory, S. 2005: Living with Chronic Illness in the Family Setting. *Sociology of Health & Illness* 27:3, 372–392.

Hacking, I. 1990: *The Taming of Chance*. Cambridge & New York: Cambridge University Press.

Hacking, I. 2006: *Kinds of People: Moving Targets* (British Academy Lecture). London.

Hauser-Schäublin, B. et al. 2001: *Der geteilte Leib: Die kulturelle Dimension von Organtransplantation und Reproduktionsmedizin in Deutschland*. Frankfurt & New York: Campus.

Hay, M.C. 2010: Suffering in a Productive World: Chronic Illness, Visibility, and the Space beyond Agency. *American Ethnologist* 37:2, 259–274.

Herzfeld, M. 2001: *Anthropology: Theoretical Practice in Culture and Society*. Malden & Oxford: Blackwell.

Hogle, L. 1999: *Recovering the Nation's Body: Cultural Memory, Medicine, and the Politics of Redemption*. Brunswick: Rutgers University Press.

Jenkins, R. et al. 2005: Matters of Life & Death: The Control of Uncertainty and the Uncertainty of Control. In: R. Jenkins et al. (eds.), *Managing Uncertainty: Ethnographic Studies of Illness, Risk and Struggle for Control*. Copenhagen: Museum Tusculanum Press, pp. 9–29.

Kalitzkus, V. 2003: *Leben durch Tod: Die zwei Seiten der Organtransplantation, eine medizinethnologische Studie*. Frankfurt: Campus.

Kaufert, P.A. 1998: Woman, Resistance, and the Breast Cancer Movement. In: M. Lock & P.A. Kaufert (eds.), *Pragmatic Women and Body Politics*. Cambridge: Cambridge University Press, pp. 287–309.

Keating, P. & A. Cambrosio 2000: Biomedical Platforms. *Configurations* 8, 337–387.

Kleinman, A. 1988: *Illness Narratives*. Boston: Beacon.

Kleinman, A. 1997: *Social Suffering*. Berkeley: University of California Press.

Kleinman, A. & D. Seeman 2000: Personal Experience of Illness. In: G.L. Albrecht et al. (eds.), *Handbook of Social Studies in Health & Medicine*. London: Sage, pp. 230–242.

Lock, M. 2000: Accounting for Disease and Distress: Morals of the Normal and Abnormal. In: G.L. Albrecht et al. (eds.), *Handbook of Social Studies in Health & Medicine*. London: Sage, pp. 259–276.

Lock, M. 2002: *Twice Dead: Organ Transplantation and the Reinvention of Death*. Berkeley: University of California Press.

Lock, M. & M. Crowley-Matoka 2008: Situating the Practice of Organ Donation in Familial, Cultural, and Political Context. *Transplantation Reviews* 22, 154–157.

Lundin, S. 2002: Creating Identity with Biotechnology: The Xenotransplanted Body as a Norm. *Public Understanding of Science* 11, 333–345.

Mongoven, A. 2003: Sharing Our Body and Blood: Organ Donation and Feminist Critiques of Sacrifice. *Journal of Medicine and Philosophy* 28:1, 89–114.

Niewöhner, J. & T. Scheffer 2010: Thickening Comparison: On the Multiple Facets of Comparability (Introduction). In: T. Scheffer & J. Niewöhner (eds.), *Thick Comparison: Reviving the Ethnographic Aspiration*. Leiden: Brill, pp. 1–15.

Ohnuki-Tierny, E. 1994: Brain Death and Organ Transplantation: Cultural Bases of Medical Technology. *Current Anthropology* 35:3, 233–254.

Parsons, T. 1951: *The Social System*. New York: Free Press.

Parsons, T. 1964: *Social Structure and Personality*. Glencoe: Free Press.

Rabinow, P. 1999: Artificiality and Enlightenment: From Sociobiology to Biosociality. In: M. Biagioli (ed.), *The Science Studies Reader*. New York: Routledge, pp. 407–416.

Rose, N. 1998: *Inventing our Selves: Psychology, Power, and Personhood*. Cambridge: Cambridge University Press.

Saltonstall, R. 1993: Healthy Bodies, Social Bodies: Men's and Women's Concepts and Practices of Health in Everyday Life. *Social Science of Medicine* 36:1, 7–14.

Schmidgunst, T. 2005: Im Netzwerk Selbsthilfe: Engagement and Aktivismus junger Parkinson Patienten. In: G. Welz et al. (eds.), *Gesunde Ansichten: Wissensaneignung medizinischer Laien*. Frankfurt: Institut für Kulturanthropologie und Europäische Ethnologie, pp. 135–153.

Sharp, L.A. 1995: Organ Transplantation as a Transformative Experience: Anthropological Insights into the Restructuring of the Self. *Medical Anthropology Quarterly* 9:3, 357–389.

Sharpe, L. & L. Curran 2006: Understanding the Process of Adjustment to Illness. *Social Science & Medicine* 62:5, 1153–1166.

Stacy, M. 1988: *The Sociology of Health and Healing*. London: Unwin Hyman.

Strathern, M. 1997: Partners and Consumers: Making Relations Visible. In: A.D. Schrift (ed.), *The Logic of the Gift: Toward an Ethic of Generosity*. New York: Routledge, pp. 292–311.

Strauss, A.L. et al. 1984: *Chronic Illness and the Quality of Life*. 2nd edition. St. Louis: Mosby.

Therborn, G. 2002: Back to Norms! On the Scope and Dynamics of Norms and Normative Action. *Current Sociology* 50:6, 863–880.

Varul, M.Z. 2010: Talcott Parsons, the Sick Role and Chronic Illness. *Body & Society* 16:2, 72–94.

Wiebel-Fanderl, O. 2003: *Herztransplantation als erzählte Erfahrung: Der Mensch zwischen kulturellen Traditionen und medizinisch-technischem Fortschritt*. Münster: Lit.

Zelizer, V.A. 2005: *The Purchase of Intimacy*. Princeton: Princeton University Press.

Katrin Amelang is a doctoral candidate at the Institute for European Ethnology, Humboldt University Berlin, Germany. She is currently completing her dissertation about the production of everyday life and normality after organ transplantation.
(katrin.amelang@staff.hu-berlin.de)

Violetta Anastasiadou-Christophidou, MD, is a paediatrician and clinical geneticist. She is head of the Clinical Genetics Department, Archbishop Makarios III Hospital and the Cyprus Institute of Neurology and Genetics in Nicosia, Cyprus.
(vanast@cing.ac.cy)

Costas S. Constantinou holds a PhD in social anthropology from the University of Bristol, UK. He is the Medical Sociology sub-theme lead and Community Placement Developer for St George's University of London Medical Programme at the University of Nicosia and an adjunct faculty member at the Open University of Cyprus. His research interests are anthropology of the human body, organ donation/transplantation, HIV/AIDS, diabetes, genetic diseases, and medicalisation.
(constantinou.c@unic.ac.cy)

Anna Johansson is a lecturer at the Department of Culture and Media Studies and HUMlab, Umeå University. Her thesis *Self-harm: An Ethnological Study of Meaning and Identity in Accounts of Cutting*, was published in 2010. Anna Johansson's research and teaching interests include feminist approaches to gender and health, discourse theory, and digital culture.
(anna.johansson@kultmed.umu.se)

Susanne Lundin is Professor of European Ethnology at Lund University, Sweden. Her recent works focus on organ transplantation and organ trafficking, cultural aspects on neurodegenerative disorders, and the impact of citizen participation on decision making in knowledge-intensive policy fields.
(susanne.lundin@kultur.lu.se)

Stefan Beck is Professor of European Ethnology at Humboldt University Berlin, Germany. He has conducted fieldwork in Cyprus and Germany, focussing on genetic screenings, organ donation and the social history of public health programs.
(stefan.beck@rz.hu-berlin.de)

POSTSOCIALISM AS A DIAGNOSTIC TOOL
Common-Sense Concepts of Power and State in Southern Poland

Anna Malewska-Szalygin

Are the common-sense concepts of power and state, used in the rural regions of Poland, manifestations of postcommunist or postsocialist mentality? Several fieldwork seasons spent in the Polish countryside let me to conclude that local concepts of power and authority used by my local informants should rather be called "postpeasant" or "posttraditional" than "postsocialist". The opinions concerning different forms of authority, as well as the state itself, shaped within the local discourse and shared by the contemporary inhabitants of rural areas of Poland, proved difficult to follow without profound understanding of traditional peasant culture, mentality and value system. Therefore, I suggest the term "postpeasant" to be applied in reference to rural communities of contemporary Poland as more accurate than the widely used term "postsocialist".

Keywords: common-sense representations, local discourses, postsocialist, postpeasant

Anthropology at Home

Any account of fieldwork conducted in Poland by a Polish ethnologist has to be preceded by a short reflection concerning its status. Is a Pole who is conducting fieldwork in Poland a native anthropologist? Is what she does anthropology at home? In times when fieldwork is explained as "sharing experience" and "negotiating sense", when we have "reflective anthropology" and the "non-transparent" researcher, conscious of her influence on the research process, the proximity between partners in fieldwork dialogue becomes an advantage. We have to be careful, however, not to be deceived by appearances. A researcher, an educated inhabitant of a large city, is perceived by farmers as a stranger, even when the language both partners communicate in is their native tongue. Sharing the same native language only creates an illusion of having something in common. Fieldwork very quickly shows how misleading this illusion happens to be, and this does not concern the dialect spoken by the older inhabitants of a rural village. The words that appear in a loose conversation concerning political matters very quickly show their multiple meanings, with the partners in the dialogue – the researcher and her interlocutor – giving the words different meanings and, moreover, with those meanings changing according to the context.

Thus, is the ethnographic research conducted by a Polish ethnologist in Poland any different from the fieldwork conducted, for example, by such American scholars as Janine Wedel, Carol Nagengast or Elisabeth Dunn? I believe the difference is fundamental. First, the researcher, for whom the language of the conversation is her native tongue, has at her disposal greater means of understanding certain linguistic nuances, different wordgames and idiomatic expressions. Second, an ethnologist educated at a Polish university knows the vast amount of ethnographic literature concerning rural inhabitants from the mid-nineteenth century till contemporary times. The literature is primarily in Polish, with the exception of the famous work by Florian Znaniecki (and William Thomas) as well as a few articles in English, for example those of Jozef Obrebski. Being acquainted with this literature, which is on the whole unknown to foreign researchers, is extremely helpful in understanding contemporary fieldwork experience. I came to understand the importance of this while conducting my own fieldwork, especially when trying to cope with the interpretation of the materials collected.

A Short Description of the Conducted Fieldwork

I conducted a research project entitled Ethnopolitology – Conversations with Polish Highlanders about Political Matters in the years 1999–2005. This took place in the villages near Nowy Targ (New Market), a town in the mountainous Podhale region in the south of Poland, at the foot of the Tatra Mountains and in the middle of the Carpathian range. It is a region known for its stability and attachment to very small farms passed down from generation to generation, and also for the two-hundred-year tradition of economic migration, forced on the farmers because of their highland farming that brought so little profit. In this region fieldwork has been conducted by many Polish ethnographers since the end of the nineteenth century, whereas from the 1970s research was conducted there by Frances Pine, an anthropologist from Cambridge University. The people chosen for study were poorly educated. They called themselves farmers although their actual source of income was temporary manual labour, often abroad. Before 1991 the majority linked work on the farm with employment in a state-run shoe factory called "Podhale", built in Nowy Targ in 1955 and extended in the 1970s. At that time it employed seven thousand workers.

Fieldwork was conducted according to Polish ethnographic tradition which is quite different when compared with British sojourns lasting for a year. It is more like American research conducted in the Indian reserves which consists of shorter stays in the places where the research is being conducted, at the same time going back there many times so as to conduct long, loosely structured conversations. My project consisted of seven weekly trips in which a group of ten undergraduate and doctoral students from Warsaw University's Institute of Ethnology and Cultural Anthropology took part.

The technique of conducting research presumed that the researcher aimed at receiving statements that would be as broad and free as possible, disciplined only by the research disposition that gave the speakers a great deal of freedom to construct their own narration, choose the appropriate expressions, comparisons and examples. The interviews were conducted in people's homes, at the marketplace, outside shops or in front of the church. The dialogues that took place between 1999 and 2000 sometimes became multivocal debates, centred around such notions as the state, different authorities, citizens, the nation, political parties, free elections, democracy and freedom. They were afterwards supplemented with conversations about their electoral preferences, and were conducted in a county-town marketplace. Those marketplace debates were extremely emotional, especially before the presidential elections in 2000, the general elections in 2001 as well as the general and presidential elections in September 2005. All the conversations were registered digitally. Over a period of six years we amassed in all about five hundred computer records of conversations that constitute very good material for the interpretation of rural village discourse on politics.[1]

The Rural Perception of Authority: Postsocialist or Postpeasant?

The media, both Polish and Western European, often characterize the political views of poorly educated people as a sign of postcommunist,[2] postsocialist mentality or as an example of the attitude defined after Alexander Zinoviev as *homo sovieticus*. The results of the fieldwork conducted in Podhale persuaded me to question those essentializing and universalizing definitions. On the basis of the research material that I have managed to put together, I hope to prove that opinions concerning different forms of authority and the state, shared and shaped in the local discourse of contemporary Polish rural villages, are primarily constructed with the help of descriptive categories characteristic of peasant culture, and it is difficult to understand them without knowledge of a farmer's traditional culture, mentality and system of values. Despite undertaking certain modernizing activities, the socialist system preserved this way of thinking, changing it so slightly that describing views of this type by means of the adjective "postsocialist" seems to be somewhat exaggerated.

I will start my argument in favour of this view by quoting Clifford Geertz who believed that the sphere of symbols and convictions was exceptionally resistant to change. He illustrated this with examples from his Indonesian studies. In interpreting Javanese funeral customs, he showed that certain notions, and expectations connected with them, illustrate a surprising stability and are transferred to new economic and political contexts that have come about as a result of Indonesia's urbanization and industrialization processes (Geertz 1973). Marshall Sahlins presented similar arguments (1995). On the basis of exotic examples, he showed that the present situation is always explained in mental categories prior to the real experience. In tribal communities, that previous knowledge was organized around myths; hence he called this *mythopraxis.* Following the thesis concerning the exceptional stability of notions, convictions and a shared system of values, it is necessary to check the truth of this opinion in connection with farming communities. In reference to the stability of notions shaped in the context of traditional farming households, for example, Nestor Garcia Canclini (1995), among others, wrote about the hybridity of the contemporary culture of Mexican peasants that links elements of traditional culture with those of modernity.

In order to argue for the stability of traditional notions in the Polish context, I must briefly characterize the peasant's view of the world. I will concentrate here on the widely known works of Robert Redfield (1956) about peasant mentality and omit the numerous publications in Polish on the subject. The peasant way of perceiving reality was partly shaped by being isolated from the external world and being strictly connected with the farmers' settled lifestyle. This resulted in them perceiving the external world with distrust, a perception created through maximizing the relationships known to them from their own small world experienced on an everyday basis. The knowledge they gained from their everyday experiences was supplemented with what they themselves imagined, which in turn led to creating stereotypes of the "other" and other notions concerning the distant reality, which was fascinating but, at the same time, frightening.

In contemporary conversations about politics we can hear echoes of such a way of drawing conclusions. The research material from Podhale clearly shows the tendency to broaden the relations of authority experienced on the farm to that of the state. For centuries, the inhabitants of the Podhale villages have been functioning within a specific context, that of a peasant farm. Organizing the farmwork, the relationships between the workers and the farmer, and the principles governing the wages received – all these experiences, which have come down over the generations – have become the basis for the way farmers perceive different authorities, both within the family and the state. However, it is worth recalling what Clifford Geertz said in his text on common knowledge (1973), that experience itself does not teach us anything. For it to pass on some message it must be interpreted in categories prior to this experience. In the discussed example, work experience on a farm, interpreted in categories of traditional peasant culture, provides the interlocutors with knowledge concerning what, in reference to those in power, relations within the state should be like today.

Peasant Perception of the State

It is worth starting any reflections on local discursive constructs by tracing the connotations of the notion "state" as they appeared in the conducted interviews. Depending on the context, it meant either state authorities in general or a combination of territorial authorities, the community inhabiting the given territory and the people in authority within that community. In the first meaning, it was simply used interchangeably with "the authorities", while in the second, it was usually explained by comparing it to a farm. I used this local simile as a source metaphor (Turner 1975), focusing on the interpretation of fieldwork materials.

From comparing the state to a farm, my informants passed smoothly to complaining about the privatization process that had taken place in Poland since 1990. The fall of state-run factories, the setting-up of private firms on the basis of mainly foreign capital, taking over the existing infrastructure sometimes put to use but often falling into ruin, were all the subject of heated criticism. How the privatization process was assessed locally, expressed in a highly emotional manner through swearing and with raised voices, using sarcasm and bitter irony, can be summarized in the often repeated sentence: "They're selling off Poland!" My informants were especially angry at the closure of the leather manufacturing complex "Podhale". It was in this factory that not only our interviewees had worked for years, but also the majority of Podhale families. Shouting out their anger and resentment, they argued: "How could they sell it?! It wasn't theirs! It belonged to the whole nation! That factory came into existence thanks to our work!"

The indignation brought about by this privatization process can be easily interpreted as proof of the attachment of the factory's former workers to the socialist ideology that would seep through to them from the factory's radio loudspeakers. I will try, however, to show that the above described attitude towards the privatization problem may be explained by referring to the peasant way of perceiving the issue of ownership and work. Ethnographical works on the rights of ownership and inheritance laws concerning a peasant farm at the turn of the twentieth century show quite a difference in principles, emphasizing at the same time that the farm either belonged to the family or to the community (Thomas & Znaniecki 1958). In this understanding of a farm – primarily the land but also the buildings and livestock – it was generally acknowledged to belong to the family, although from the legal point of view, it was often owned by the person who farmed the land. Even if, according to the inheritance law, the farm was passed down to one person, according to custom and to what was perceived as morally right, it was seen as belonging to the whole family. The farmer who was a good manager, who bought up land, extended the house or invested in more outbuildings, enriched the whole family, also his children and future grandchildren. The farmer who sold off his land would be depriving the present and future generations of the achievements of their father, grandfather and great-grandfather. If we were to look at the privatization process through the peasants' conviction concerning their property rights and were to refer the same criterion to the state, their indignation becomes fully understandable. Looking at it from the farmer's point of view, the government in Poland after 1989 acted like a bad farmer, like a squanderer, selling off what belonged to the nation, or, to be more exact, what had been achieved through the work of the nation. Proof of this line of interpretation may be our interviewees' statements, among which we often heard: "A nation within the state is like a family at home." "The state is like a farm that belongs to the whole nation." These were usually brought to a conclusion with the highly indignant statement: "How could they sell the shoe factory if it came into existence thanks to our work?!" "It wasn't theirs, so how could they sell it?!" Although in such exclamations we can of course see the influence of socialist propaganda, I would prefer to see the attitude described above as having much older roots.

Transferring to the state the relationships known from the farm explains many other complaints about the transformation process. The interviewees often said: "There is no justice in Poland today." They would then explain that what they were thinking about was the lack of justice connected with remuneration for their work, work done both today and in the past, which was the basis for working out their pensions. The market economy theory of remuneration is calculated according to demand, the changing prices of products and many other factors, among which there is no place for such moral categories as honesty or justice. Looking at it in this way, complaining about today's lack of justice in remuneration may be perceived as a sign of postcommunist nostalgia, as longing for the ideal of social justice that had been popularized by socialist propaganda. I believe, however, that such a time perspective is too short. Florian Znaniecki presents the understanding of justice in folk culture by describing the relation between employing farmhands and help on the farm (Thomas & Znaniecki 1958). The farmhand was to do his work in an honest manner, in other words, as well as he could. The farmer employing him was to pay him honestly, in such a way that the worker could support himself as well as his whole family. As the example presented by Znaniecki shows, fair remuneration is such that it will support the worker and his family. If from this perspective we look at the economic situation of many farmers and labourers from the transformation period, we can clearly see that it was not possible for them to support themselves and their families. Thus, following the above described train of thought, the remuneration was not fair and this justified the general statement that "there is no justice in Poland today."

Often in the conversations from 1999–2001, we could hear such statements as: "Work should be assured!" The argument was that when so many manual labourers could not find work in Poland and had to look for employment abroad, it was a sign of defeat on the part of the government. The expectation that the state will assure employment obviously seems to have been inherited from socialism, from the times when the state was the largest employer. However, if we look at the relationships governing a traditional farm, the expectation that the farmer will divide the work so that everybody has a job to do is the logical consequence of the assumptions presented in the example of a good farmer. Referring once more to the comparison between the state and a farm, we may notice that the responsibilities of the state authorities, which result from this analogy, are similar to the responsibilities of the farmer. The former should make sure their citizens are employed in the same way as the latter organizes the work on his farm. If everybody was employed and people did not think about looking for work abroad, Poland would only benefit from it.

Local Perceptions of Authority

Applying the metaphor "manager of the country" on the government very often took on the form of a complaint: "Poland today has no manager! It's just drifting along! There's a need for good management!" Such comments, appearing in nearly every conversation we held in Nowy Targ, confirm the view that people living in the countryside imagine an ideal government through the example of a good farmer and manager, broadly described in literary works dealing with peasant culture. Applying this farming example to the assessment of those in the government has far-reaching consequences, for example the dislike of a representative government in contrast to their liking for autocratic power. In the conversations we held, criticism of Polish members of parliament was very frequent. Utterances that were highly emotional and full of vulgar abuse pointed towards them pursuing their personal interests and profiting from the situation; the informants touched upon nepotism, and many other shortcomings such as drinking too much or leading immoral lives. These outbursts of anger would often end with how one could exterminate parliament with the help of rather extreme methods (such as gassing everybody, blowing them up or hanging them), which can be seen as unquestionable proof of their dislike of this type of government.

Their complaints concerning members of parliament can be seen as having been inherited from communism, with its one-party system and the removal of the general public from having any real influence on whom they vote for.[3] However, continuing our interpretation of the fieldwork material through reference to traditional peasant culture, we can look at it in a different way. In one of the utterances, we came across something that explained the dislike for a representative government in farming categories.

An older farmer, commenting on the economic situation in Poland in the year 2000 said: "They manage the country in ... you know ... like a farmer who doesn't keep an eye on his farmhands. The farmhands will sell off bloody everything! They'll sell off Poland in the same way!" Looking from the perspective of a peasant farm, its true manager is the farmer who inherits this job from those who came before him. There is no place here for eligibility or for collectivity. Power that has its origins in choice, which is additionally collective, appears as a substitute for real power. If the country does not have a real manager, the nation will be governed by farmhands, just like in the description of parliamentary authority according to farming categories.

In the opinion of our Nowy Targ interviewees, a democratic government's biggest drawback is its lack of effectiveness, which is connected with many people being involved in the decision-making process and in the blurring of responsibility. That is why in describing the ideal of good government, it was stressed that those in power should be strong and decisive and should rule with an iron fist. In our highland conversations, the nation was often compared to a flock of sheep and the government to their shepherd. Sometimes the nation was compared to children and state authority to a father. Describing society as sheep or children is rather distant from the Enlightenment concept of social consensus that is based on the liberal assumption that everybody has a share, through his representatives, in taking decisions that concern common affairs. The farming way of thinking about the government seems to be quite a long way away from the concept of Jean-Jacques Rousseau and other thinkers who created the foundations for representational democracy in Europe.

The lack of correspondence between these two ways of thinking can be seen especially clearly in the examples of a good ruler as presented by our Nowy Targ interviewees. Introduced examples were a parade of historical figures associated with authoritarian strength, power held by one person and assuring the welfare of his subjects. The last Austrian-Hungarian Emperor Franz Josef was often recalled, as was Marshal Jozef Pilsudski, head of the Polish state after World War I, and Edward Gierek, the first secretary of the Communist Party in the 1970s. The times when they "reigned" were seen by our interviewees to be periods of stability and prosperity in the countryside. There also appeared other, much more controversial, figures, such as Adolf Hitler or Augusto Pinochet, representing the idea of uncompromising power and those who firmly established and consolidated order. It is interesting, however, that among the names listed, Stalin never appeared. The key to the choice of people quoted as examples of good rulers was the category of order. According to our interviewees, it was order, which assured the farmer stability and security, that justified the ruler's firmness, severity, and even cruelty. On the contrary, any upheaval associated with revolution or war, that is, with the weakening of the state, awakened fear, which can be easily understood if we look at it from the farmer's point of view. Stability is essential if a farm is to bring profit.

Among the Podhale examples of a good ruler, first place was given to Pope John Paul II, called the Holy Father by our interviewees. He was the embodiment of what they perceived as perfection. They would stress that his papal authority did not come from human choice. Although our interviewees were aware of the fact that the pope was elected by a conclave of cardinals, as far as John Paul II was concerned, they believed that this honour had been granted by God and had been preceded by signs revealing divine will.[4] It is difficult in the twenty-first century to state that rural inhabitants are expecting a ruler who would be anointed by divine will, but utterances such as "There still hasn't appeared anybody who would rule with a steady hand" can be heard, which suggests that a good ruler is assumed to be specially predisposed to perform certain duties. What is expected most is charisma or, as they said, power from above. Our interviewees often stressed that John Paul II was a perfect ruler because he was given such great power that he could have influence over the political situation of the whole world. This could clearly be seen in the sentence: "Our Holy Father brought down the Berlin Wall, overthrew Communism and united Europe."

The Nowy Targ examples of a good ruler quoted above revealed the acceptance of this type of rule which, quoting Max Weber, can be called traditional, also charismatic, and quoting Michel Foucault, pastoral or patriarchal.

Quoting the example of John Paul II may suggest that in the image of the world which our Nowy Targ interviewees had, power is associated with goodness. This was, however, only the case when the conversations were about the positive models of power. When conversations concerned power in the reality, it was very often described in absolutist terms, and as being diabolical. The following sentence clearly presents the satanist provenience of real power: "You know who's now in authority?! The Devil!" The pope represented a heavenly ideal, while the earthly reality of authority was perceived as its opposite. This brings to mind the differentiation made by St Augustine between the perfect divine state and the imperfect state created by people.

Reflections on those in authority between 1999 and 2005 primarily stressed their alienation, which brought about an ambivalent reaction. On the one hand, it contains an element of fascination, while on the other, danger. What the Podhale people thought about politicians was also constructed on the basis of fear and fascination. The government was seen by our interviewees as being hostile towards simple, hard-working people. The following sentence reveals this very well: "They're sitting there in that parliament every day, sitting and debating over whom they can fucking get at. And of course it's always the farmer, the worker whose arse they'll go for! They'll never do it to themselves!" In this rather inelegant manner, they commented on the work of members of parliament and on fiscal policy.

In observing this hostility, we were provoked to reflect on the reasons for such a state of affairs. The answers formulated by our Nowy Targ interviewees to the fundamental question concerning why it was so bad, boiled down to accusing the politicians of being strangers, nationally or as far as their social class was concerned. The suggestions of ethnic foreignness contained the constantly repeated statement: "Now there are only Jews in the government." Appearing in nearly every answer, "Jews are in charge" symbolically expressed the conviction that there would be a foreign government in the service "of another nation" – as they said. The word "Jews" used in this context did not refer to the Jews who used to live in Nowy Targ and in the surrounding area, whom many of our interviewees still remembered from the times of their childhood. It also did not refer to the followers of Judaism or to the citizens of the state of Israel. The term "Jew" in the context of conversations about contemporary state authority simply served to symbolically stress the "otherness" of the politicians.

This "otherness" was also sometimes described by the word *pany* (plebeian plural form for mister/master). To understand the symbolic dimension of this term, it is necessary to know that according to our interviewees, the Polish nation is divided into two basic categories: "those who work" and "those who don't need to work," whereas the verb "work" here implies manual labour. This refers to the social class division into *pany* and *chamy* (plebeian form for the contradiction masters–peasants, derived from the biblical name of Noah's son Ham) or "of the master" and "of the peasant" that has been described in historical and sociological publications. In today's Podhale rustic discourse, the historical category of *pany* is doing very well, whereas I never heard my interviewees describe themselves as peasants, never mind rustics. When speaking about themselves, they would say "we – farmers" or "we – simple, poor people", or even "we – those who work". In as far as the category "we" was pretty obvious to them, the category "they" (*pany*, "Jews", "those who don't need to work") was fuzzy and vague. Not much was said about "them".

The term *pany* often appeared when our interviewees presented what they imagined the life of people in power to be like. They would then say: "They're living like lords. At night they're drinking in casinos, having a good time with the girls, and fiddlers are playing below their hotel windows." This utterance, like many similar ones, describes the fascinating side of authority: prosperity and luxury. The interviewees thought the life of politicians to be pleasant but immoral. According to them, it was only the life of a person doing hard manual labour that was honest. The life of politicians was dishonest.

The Rural Understanding of the Notion "Politics"

Reflecting on what politicians are concerned with led us, researchers, to the discovery that the word "politics" has a totally different meaning locally than it has in public discourse. Politics may be defined as the process of setting and achieving social goals (Swartz, Turner & Tuden 1966), whereas the media may also use the word "politics" to describe a certain sphere of discourse. For our Podhale interviewees, though, the word meant the jobs performed by people in authority. They saw politics as only a certain type of work, or rather as the non-work of politicians. They would say: "It's not normal work, it's just something they do." Sometimes there would appear other local explanations: "Politics is just talking about nothing" or "Politics is just something to do for those who don't have to work." All these utterances stress that politics is a form of activity that one can hardly call work. Real work comes together with the ethos that is part of this notion in peasant culture. This activity brings in money, guarantees prosperity, but it is seen as taking place in a lazy and immoral manner. This can be observed very clearly in how our interviewees compared politics to gambling and prostitution. Very often we would hear that "politics is a whore." In rural villages, prostitution is perceived as a way to get rich without working – an easy way and completely immoral. The reason for applying such a comparison was to stress that what politicians do can be characterized in this way. Referring to a prostitute in the context of conversations on politics also had another meaning. From the peasant perspective, prostitution is seen as an exceptional form of dishonesty that is based on pretending love for the sake of profit. This aspect of the matter also concerned what the locals thought about politicians declaring their wish to act for the common good, while under the surface of beautiful words was only their desire to make money. That is why comparing politics to a whore is, according to our Nowy Targ interviewees, a very good description of what they see as the very core of what politicians do and is the most concise conclusion of the reflections on what politics is.

The Folk Roots of Contemporary Perceptions of the Government and the State

There were many other extremely surprising comparisons and statements that appeared during our Podhale interviews. It was only when we began to consider them in the category of folk culture that they could be understood, as was also the case with many forms of complaint, anger, insults and vulgar expletives. The fact that knowledge about folk culture turned out to be a point of reference facilitating a deeper interpretation of the materials is yet one more argument in favour of the view that the way of thinking described here has not been inherited from socialist times. That is why I believe that the expression postcommunist or postsocialist mentality is not appropriate enough here to describe rural perceptions of the government and the state and should be exchanged for something else. If we were to keep "mentality", which in ethnology is an extremely essentializing and universalizing word, it is necessary to qualify it with a different adjective. Keeping to the convention that is fashionable today, that is to add the prefix "post" to different adjectives, we could suggest "postpeasant". This would be in conjunction with the term proposed by Clifford Geertz (1962). We could also use "posttraditional" that has been suggested more recently by Juraj Buzalka (2007).

In contemporary local discourse, the categories of traditional reflection on the reality have been mixed with later ones, with selectively accepted bits and pieces of socialist ideology. Besides these ideological components, we can also hear echoes of national ideals that were promoted in the Podhale villages by elementary schools during the interwar period and continued in their own specific way by teachers in the Polish People's Republic. In our interviews we could discern the teachings of the Catholic Church that have come down over the centuries and which would include elements of theological thought (e.g. St Augustine on a divine as well as civil state) passed on to the highlanders by generations of rural parish priests. From small particles of the above mentioned systems of ideas a system of views has been formed over the years, which is striking in its eclectic and heterogeneous nature. It supplies rural thinkers and commentators with a cohesive image of the world, making it easier for them to find their own place in a dynamically changing reality. In order to make a detailed study of the local "archaeology of knowledge", it would be necessary to conduct an analysis according to Foucault's principles of studying the history of ideas. However, even less detailed research on common peasant knowledge permits the claim that socialist ideas do not seem to be significant enough here to define this type of reflection on reality as postsocialist. If one of the notional components were to be described as basic, it would be the way of perceiving and describing the world that is characteristic of traditional peasant culture.

The Adequacy of the Postsocialism Category

In conclusion it would be worth taking into consideration the appropriateness of the term "postsocialism" as a diagnostic tool. I agree with Jill Owczarzak who suggests that "<postsocialism> has been used as a geographic label, not an analytic category, in contrast to <postcolonialism>, which has a rich history as a theoretical paradigm" (2009: 4). That is probably why attempts have been made to refer research on postsocialism to theories better grounded in anthropology, for example anthropology of development (Brandtstädter 2007). However, what has turned out to be extremely fruitful has been the results of the postcolonial studies put forward by Katherine Verdery (2002). According to her suggestion, the category "postsocialism" is not so much an analytical tool as an element of Western discourse and practices in inventing the East. Applying this notion is, according to Verdery, a continuation of Western rhetoric from the times of the Cold War that accentuated the stereotypical image of the East for the needs of the contemporaneous ideological war. Today the postsocialism category belongs to the post-Cold War discourse that presented the East according to the European manner of constructing the Orient. Michał Buchowski (2006) writes very clearly about the "orientalization" of the Eastern Bloc by Western analysts and commentators, stressing that this process started earlier than during the Cold-War period. He points towards its Enlightenment roots (Wolff 1994).

Buchowski also points to the fact that not only is external discourse, which presents the East as it is perceived from the Western perspective, orientalizing in nature. An equally significant phenomenon is "domestic orientalism" (2006: 467), which describes the orientalizing discourse and practice of the Polish elites, especially the media that dominate Polish political discourse. The elitist "hegemonic discourse" (2006: 476) marginalizes voices coming from the working classes, creating not only the "voice" but also the identity of the uneducated members of society, including farmers, as people not able to cope in a reality shaped by a freemarket economy, privatization and democratization. In this way, writes Buchowski, the "exotic other" becomes the "stigmatized brother" (2006: 463) in Polish public discourse.

Research conducted according to the ethnographic fieldwork method may be a departure from the discursive practice of "domestic orientalization". This technique forces the researcher to become immersed in local rural discourse, with its specific language and characteristic way of verbalizing opinions. The ethnologist, being a participant of both the "hegemonic discourse" and peasant conversations on politics, presenting a far-reaching openness, can understand how her village interviewees construct their narration on the government, state, nation, as well as on themselves. The ethnologist describes these local discursive constructs by applying categories that belong to the methodology used by the social sciences. She places them within a narrative constructed by her which is formulated in a language that is either academic or destined for the general public. In order to do this, she has to reconstruct local discursive constructs in the elite discourse. Thanks to such an operation, the marginalized voice of the rural commentators has a chance to appear in public discourse. The ethnological immersion in the underprivileged discourses erodes the "orientalizing" categories such as postcommunist, postsocialist or the term *homo sovieticus* that belong to the hegemonic discourse.

Notes

1 This article was translated from Polish by Aniela Korzeniowska.

2 The adjective postcommunist (or communist) during the times of the Polish People's Republic, which was then reserved for the discourse of Polish opposition activists and Western commentators, is now used in narration that is critical of the past system. The term postsocialist (or socialist), functioning in the official discourse of that past system's authorities and in the then public media, now appears in narrations that are more favourable towards the old system.

3 During the times of the Polish People's Republic voting lists were prepared by the Communist Party and other parties that were linked to it. Voters were advised to vote without crossing anybody out, which meant that the list remained in its original form.

4 The sign from God that our interviewees had in mind had been given to the chosen person during the coronation ceremony of Our Lady of Ludzmierz in 1963 (Ludzmierz is the main Marian shrine of the Podhale region). During the procession, the figure leant over and the sceptre fell out of Our Lady's hand. It was caught by Bishop Karol Wojtyla, who was later to become Pope John Paul II. Our Nowy Targ interviewees interpreted this event as a sign from God. Karol Wojtyla was thus destined for the highest position in the Church and the highlanders were the first to have this revealed to them.

References

Brandtstädter, S. 2007: Transitional Spaces: Postsocialism as a Cultural Process. Introduction. *Critique of Anthropology*, vol. 27, no. 2, pp. 131–145.

Buchowski, M. 2006: The Specter of Orientalism in Europe: From Exotic Other to Stigmatized Brother. *Anthropological Quarterly*, vol. 79, no. 3, pp. 463–482.

Buzalka, J. 2007: *Nation and Religion: The Politics of Commemoration in South East Poland*. Berlin: Lit Verlag.

Garcia Canclini, N. 1995: *Hybrid Cultures: Strategies for Entering and Leaving Modernity*. Minneapolis: University of Minnesota Press.

Geertz, C. 1962: Studies in Peasant Life: Community and Society. In: Bernard J. Siegel (ed.), *Biennial Review of Anthropology 1961*. Stanford: Stanford University Press.

Geertz, C. 1973: *Interpretation of Cultures*. New York: Basic Books.

Owczarzak, J. 2009: Introduction: Postcolonial Studies and Postsocialism in Eastern Europe. *Focaal – European Journal of Anthropology*, vol. 53, pp. 3–19.

Redfield, R. 1956: *Peasant Society and Culture: An Anthropological Approach to Civilization*. Chicago: University of Chicago Press.

Sahlins, M. 1995: *How 'Natives' Think: About Captain Cook, for example*. Chicago: University of Chicago Press.

Swartz, M., V. Turner & A. Tuden 1966: *Political Anthropology*. Chicago: Aldine.

Thomas, W.I. & F. Znaniecki 1958: *The Polish Peasant in Europe and America*. New York: Dover Publications.

Turner, V. 1975: *Dramas, Fields, and Metaphors: Symbolic Action in Human Society*. Ithaca, New York: Cornell University Press.

Verdery, K. 2002: Introduction. In: C. Hann (ed.), *Postsocialism: Ideals, Ideologies, and Practices in Eurasia*. London & New York: Routledge.

Wolff, L. 1994: *Inventing Eastern Europe*. Stanford: Stanford University Press.

Anna Malewska-Szalygin is an assistant professor at the Institute of Ethnology and Cultural Anthropology, University of Warsaw. Her fields of study are peasant common knowledge, rural discourses about local and central authorities, power, the state, nation and democracy. Her fieldwork terrain is Poland. Her recent publications are: Local Discourse on Matters of the State: A Podhale Case (in L. Mroz & A. Posern-Zielinski, eds., *Exploring Home, Neighboring and Distant Cultures*, Warsaw: DiG, 2008), and Market View of the Polish Political Scene (*Anthropology Matters*, No. 1, 2006, www.anthropologymatters.com/journal/2006-1).
(anmalsz@wp.pl)